Big Church, Little Church, Let Me In

365 Days With God

Tiffany Luv Browning

Copyright © 2019 by Tiffany Browning
All Rights Reserved

No part of this publication may be reproduced, distributed, or transmitted in any form or by any means, including photocopying, recording, or other electronic or mechanical methods, without the prior written permission of the publisher, except in the case of brief quotations embodied in critical reviews and certain other noncommercial uses permitted by copyright law.

Table of Contents

Chapter One 1

Chapter One, Chapter One: The Start Over 21

Chapter Two: Open House 29

Chapter Three: Phoebe 39

Chapter Four: Kyle and the Church Bully 51

Chapter Five: God's *Will* 57

Chapter Six: Daniel Fast-21 Days of Prayer 63

Chapter Seven: The Instant Message 71

Chapter Eight: True Salvation 83

Chapter Nine: The Prodigal Daughter & The Wayward Child 93

Chapter Ten: Revival 105

Chapter Eleven 111

Chapter One

James 1:17 NIV Every good and perfect gift is from above, coming down from the Father of the heavenly lights, who does not change like shifting shadows.

What if I told you that everything you've ever thought about God, and the Son, were a lie?

What if I told you it was the truth?

Where does our truth fall?

I will tell you that it is somewhere in between the pages of a book written by man and inspired by our Creator and the story of our Savior. It is in the Gospel of Jesus Christ where our answers lay.

When God asked me to put everything down that I was carrying, I tried. But what He put on my heart to write; I didn't want to write. I had written 239 pages of this book already when He asked me to start over. I think He knew I was trying to sugar coat the message. What I started to write wasn't the truth He asked me to write. I was trying to reach an audience that I wanted to reach, not that He wanted to reach. His message is so powerful and His patience so gentle, that here we are. He knows I am a stubborn child, so He waits patiently, because He also sees my obedience in my stubbornness. And He understands my longing and yearning to please Him and how it gets washed away in my longing to please my fellow person. So many of you who have spent your lifetime running from a spiritual calling understand exactly what I am trying to say.

It tends to take some of us longer than others, but when we are still and we lean in to what He is telling us, it eventually becomes our life mission. It may scare you, and it may seem like it's controversial, but if you've read any part of the story of Jesus, well, you know sometimes it takes courage to go against the social grain to reset our spirituality and focus back on Him.

I wasn't always a Christian. I was always "spiritual" in the most proverbial and ostentatious manner. I'll tell you my story and hopefully it helps you along your journey to your own salvation. I've always been a storyteller, either by words, drawing, or photographs. Artistic flair is pumping through my veins just as much as the blood that keeps my body thriving. Those of us born with the itch to create will never be able to escape the silent prison that others struggle to understand. But if I understand anything from the Bible, I understand that is exactly why so many of us are called into the mission field. It is why He chooses us. We are the clay between His hands. When we allow Him to start to soften and warm us up, we bend and mold easily. We are ordered to continue creating new ways to spread His word and love.

About 5 weeks ago I was having coffee with a friend. She is a new friend and one who has been called to spread God's message in a unique way. She's been called to the entertainment industry and it was interesting to see how our similar personalities were easily melded together as we chatted over coffee and landed on a subject that we were both struggling with or had struggled with in the past.

What happens after you are saved? What happens when you find yourself serving the church more than you are serving God?

How do you cope with the doubt and obedience the church finds rebellious with the message that God has very plainly asked you to deliver to His people? What if God calls you to do something different than your church is doing at the moment? We both reflected on women we knew who were struggling with doubt and their loyalty to God and the legalities of serving in the church life. And it wasn't just a few women, it was a lot of women. In the middle of a revival they were leaving the church or taking a break from the church in droves. I wanted to know why, even though deep down I already knew the answer.

We are two very different women on two very different paths with very different backgrounds.

I am a born-again Christian. She was raised in a Christian home.

I was never the popular type; I was a rebel child. I am a wayward daughter who took a long time coming home with a past riddled and stained with horrific abuse. She is everything good and kind and righteous, raised in a Godly, normal and healthy family. And yet, here we are at the exact same spiritual crossroads. We are Sandy and Rizzo, which some of you will get. Only, I don't sing in public. And I quit smoking a few years ago.

We are dealing with some of the same struggles. We had the same nudge from God. We both know we are called into the ministry to save women and girls from a life absence of their Creator and our Savior, Jesus Christ. We both love all types of people. We can feel God calling women into His ministry only to get frustrated and lost on their way.

This is where it may get emotional for me, and for you too.

I wanted to be Sandy. I wanted to be nice and sweet and untainted. I wanted to be innocent. I wanted people to look at me and see who I was on the inside, and yet, I was Rizzo on the outside. Because it was easier to be her through my pain. There are so many of you out there right now reading that sentence over and over because you get it. I wanted to be the girl all the teachers liked. I wanted to be the girl with the pretty clothes and the nice family. I wanted so badly to be normal. I wanted to be the girl who could just keep her mouth shut at injustice, and smile and wave at the camera. I wanted to be calm, cool, and collected.

And here I am, at forty years old, and have spent the better part of the last 6 or so months struggling with it again.

Why?

Because, church.

Legalities. Money. Injustice. Sadness.

Rules and hypocrisy. Stress. Doubt. Frustration. You name it, I've dealt with it. After the buzz of salvation wears off and you clean up those sinners' goggles you wore for so long, you struggle to hang on to the rod because someone on the other end is pulling it. And they are pulling it hard. What happens to us during that first-year struggle?

Because so many of us sit in church and hear the words being preached and we do not see it being lived through leadership or our neighbors. We want so badly for someone to share their testimony that doesn't start with them falling off of the church family band wagon and then hopping back on with a Sunday Sandy smile. We want to see and hear and feel the raw pain of a born-again Christian. We don't want to see the social media feeds filled with advertising or the latest church gadgets or marketing material. We want to be moved by Believer's who are hurting or are in pain. I think some of us want our church to do something without expecting recognition for it. Show me your leadership and your community, tell me their story, and I'll tell you where your new members have disappeared to in the last 6 or 8 months. How much time are you spending with your newly saved women? Are you copying and pasting the same message to them? Are you tight-rope walking on the excuse that there isn't enough time in the day, or that one mission is more important than encouraging and walking new members through the first year of salvation? Do you stumble through prayers or words of encouragement and fall back on, well...just read your Bible? You can be the best preacher in the world but when the minute sincerity wears off, it shows.

Being a new Christian is hard. It isn't all jazz hands and Bible verses for us. It's a daily battle with Satan himself. It is the most epic, bloody, painful hardship you can endure, spiritually. It is constant turmoil between old self and new self and everything in between. It is the struggle of remembering sins and how to turn away from temptation. It is coping with the backlash of those around you who want the old you back. It is dragging your kids to church again while they grumble and complain because they want their old life back. It's biting back tears when leadership walks by you and doesn't even acknowledge who you are. It's being called to serve time and time again, and not once, being told thank you other than a blanket congregation message. And then, being told you're being childish or selfish because you feel like it's cold and impersonal. You see so many wandering the halls of your church every single day and yet in an instant so many of them vanish. People want people. It's the core of our heart's existence. God knows this. It's why He created man and woman in the very beginning. So that we wouldn't be lonely. He knew what we would crave between our birth and our death. That is why we are called to serve in our community, because people simply want people.

It isn't Sandy or Rizzo, but somewhere in between the two. Being sugary sweet only lasts so long for some of us. We want to see those who are coming through the doors raw and broken. We want to serve the lost and lonely. We want to see leadership getting their hands dirty with the homeless and drug addicts, not just giving away fancy marketing. Show it to us. Show us your scars. Show us the aftermath of a wayward child. Show us how you are washing the feet of Christ. Take away the glitz and glamour of it. Most importantly, do it in your hometown. Do it where it matters the most. Jesus worked in the town He was in. He knew the epicenter of change starts at home. He understood that home truly is where the heart is, but more importantly that He was the church. Not the other way around.

A lot of people will read this and say, "Well you're just salty because _____". But that isn't it. I'm broken. So many of us are hard-core broken. We are broken because of drugs, alcohol, abortion, or poverty. We are broken emotionally, physically and sexually because of awful abuse. We are broken from divorce, rape, a failing school system and government policies. We are broken because of divisive hatred and a media that keeps driving the wedge even harder. We cry out to God to save us at church. For whatever reason gets us there, He sends His Son to save us. He meets us where we are.

What you find when you peel back the layers of this revival are women who try and live for the church and the church alone. It ignites an entirely different and more difficult battle than you can ever imagine. Every social media post of your favorite gospel preacher is them sitting poolside spewing Bible verses or scrambling to catch their next flight while you struggle to keep your kid from relapsing on heroine again. Every sermon starts to turn into someone with their hand out asking for the money you can't seem to come up with in the name of a tithe. Or maybe you're a middle-class mom, you've given every time they've asked, you serve with a smile on your face, you buy the tee shirts and the conference tickets...and then you tell them no, once. And never hear from someone again. The sermons on serving with a smile cause you to bite back hot painful tears because you were serving. You were...and you stopped.

Because you are exhausted. Because you can't see anything clearly anymore. You've lost sight of Jesus and He is crying to you to look up, at Him. Go directly to Him. He knows before you do what is coming. He warns us about becoming burned out by the church and yet, we get caught up in humanity and do it anyway.

It isn't because you are weak. And it isn't because God is asking you to serve Him to the point of exhaustion.

I want you to read this verse again. And then I want you to read every single red-letter word coming from Jesus Christ in your Bible. I want you to see how His disciples loved Him so much and why He chose them. He CHOSE them because they were broken. Because they had the ability and the nerve and the hearts to create a fellowship with and for their Creator. He chose them because when it was hard, they could stand up and tell the truth. He chose them because He fell in love with them, too. Just like He has fallen in love with you. He chose them because they were all broken, they drank wine, they laughed and cried and stumbled through their humanity and that is what He fell in love with.

I'll start from the beginning so you can see who I am and where I came from. It is my prayer that this helps you to pick yourself up off of the ground spiritually and remember why He pulled you from your own fire and hell. I want you to remember that serving Him doesn't always mean serving the church every time they ask you. I want you to know that He knows and will prompt you when you need to center yourself in His word and ignore what some of us like to call the front row parrots of the church. And you will learn to find where you fit in, in your church. Whether it's big or small. There is a place for you in God's house. It might take a little blood, sweat, and tears to get there, but you will find your place among those in the throne room.

There's room for all types of women in the church. If we don't start teaching our girls this lesson, they will get swallowed up by the pressure to live for humans as opposed to living for God. They will walk away tossing their hands up and miss the One who loves them the most. They will miss divine strength and hope and love.

Jesus doesn't judge the woman at the well. It's such a famous story for so many preaching the Gospel to fall back on. He sits with her. He listens to her. Even though He already knows her story. And yet, He shows her love anyway. He doesn't count her sins or tell her she's isn't good enough. It's one simple act of kindness and respect that often gets missed. But that story is important because it shows us that Jesus was human. It is also important because it begs the question, how many times have you sat with the woman at the well?

James 1:17 NIV

Every good and perfect gift is from above, coming down from the Father of the heavenly lights, who does not change like shifting shadows.

God knows your heart. He knows who you are. He created us all so differently and yet similar at the same time. He wants us to know His people by sight. He wants to see us not just talking about the word of God but living it and stumbling through it so that you learn to rely on His sovereign grace. He doesn't want us to condemn, it is our job to love. He wants us to tell the truth and say the hard things, because it's the only way to realign with the word of God. The way is the truth.

Sermons are amazing. But if they are clothed in jazz hands the cloudy message can leave a woman feeling doubtful and sad. Here is something that isn't touched upon enough.

Doubt. We don't talk about it enough.

But if there were no doubt, if God didn't understand doubt, how could we learn to rely on faith so heavily? Doubt is the pre-cursor to a miracle. Doubt is what keeps us coming right back to Him. We look back to our Father in order to be able to move ahead. It's like a tiny toddler walking for the first time, or wandering from her parents, she glances back to make sure they are in fact watching and guiding and encouraging. It is how we seek His word and guidance. It is why the answers lie in the pages of the Bible. It's an inner strength that no amount of seminary can teach you. It's an inner voice that doesn't require some fancy degree. He buried it deep inside of all of us. The Sandy's and the Rizzo's, and every girl's personality in between.

And somehow, we end up under the same roof. Look around you. Every woman in your church has something to teach you. You may not like it, you may not want to hear it, you may think you're so far into your "journey" that you are too mature to learn anymore, but no. Just no, as so many like to say. Every single person who walks through those church doors has a divine purpose. We get so caught up looking down our noses once we think we've mastered something that we ignore the small still voice in someone else. We can easily lose sight of those who are, new to whatever we may have been doing a while.

Before I was saved, I used to go see a psychic every six months or so. She was kind and informative. And most of the time, she was right. I remember her telling me it wouldn't be until my 5th book that I would find purpose or success in writing. I'll let you guess what book number this one is. In her own way, God used her to speak to me. He is funny like that. Yet if I tell that story in church, I would have to interchange the word psychic with "prophet" and then the message is lost in translation. His message is lost. God will use every situation and every person who crosses your path in some significant way. He will take everyday coincidence's and use that to warm you up and mold you like putty in His hands.

He is the artist. He is our Creator. And if I've learned anything this last year, it's His grace that gives us a purpose and His love that helps us with our strength. And sometimes He absolutely asks us to do some really hard things. But it is never without His support and love.

You are His church. It is so easy to get lost in the movie of life. But remember that all of the characters are important, and He loves one just as much as the next. Our director has already completed this script, and all is not lost. Well, except the enemy.

We are sharing the same story so let's get cozy. I'll be the Riz to your Sandy. There is room for everyone at the Lord's table. Straighten up those wings and I'll scoot my seat right over for you.

I'm going to let you be a fly on the salvation wall. I want you to see our story and feel just how close to a spiritual breakdown I came. I need you to see yourself, your daughter, your family in our story. I need you to recognize a friend who may be struggling. I want you to reach out to her, text her, call her...ask her why she stopped attending the church. Why is she sad? What happened?

We all need to be reading the same book together, maybe not on the same page at the same time, but if we understand that, we can help each other along this journey. Remember, we rely on Him, we help one another.

It is our divine created purpose from our God. He is telling us to never leave a battle buddy behind.

Writing Time: Tuesday January 2nd, 2018

Mathew 18:12 says:

NIV

"What do you think? If a man owns a hundred sheep, and one of them wanders away, will He not leave the ninety-nine on the hills and go to look for the one that wandered off?"

The entry to the psychiatric unit was dark and empty. The silence was chilling to the bone. It was New Year's Day and there wasn't a soul insight. *"You can't have a breakdown on New Year's Day",* I thought to myself. I mean, the way you spend New Year's holidays are indicative of the rest of the year, right?

What a way to ring in our new year. We had experienced the great head lice scare of 2017, the bed bug scare because my kids had stayed somewhere where they were active, we sent son number one off to the Army, son number two acted out after son number one moved away, I lost my job in the summer after an immigration and human resources debacle and there was the day Alex died.

2018 wasn't proving to be any more forgiving or fortuitous than the previous year.

The only good thing was I had managed to continue to be successful at was to not smoke cigarettes. It was a daunting and tough addiction to constantly battle for the better part of 20 years.

My son and I made the biting negative nine degree walk across the parking lot slowly, but the important thing was we made it. We walked through the halls and no one was there, it was entirely empty. The air was frigid and stagnant. I was angry, tired, hungry and sad. He was angry, tired, hungry and sad. The heels of his boots echoed throughout the empty halls. His constant cursing was booming throughout them too.

"Are you freaking kidding me?" I mumbled. I stood there trying to find some form of life. It was a comical way to start our new year, that was for sure.

He followed me back out to the parking lot, and we climbed back into the luxury sedan we had worked so hard to buy. It was what I had always thought I wanted.

We sat in silence.

"Let's just go home..." he muttered hatefully. His breath smelled terrible and his greasy blonde hair was a mop on the top of his head. I didn't even know when he had showered last. I didn't know when he had eaten either.

We spent the next two hours on speaker phone with his father and step-father while our son screamed and cussed at all of us. The night before had been the same. We had spent it talking him out of the proverbial mental health breakdown tree. He kicked my dash, he punched my window, he cussed and smoked, and he cried. The hard cry.

Then we sat in silence and as we did, a small part of me was hoping someone would call the police department when he was so loud, just so I could get help getting him in. How was I supposed to drag a six-foot man-child into the hospital? Around three o'clock we sauntered soberly through the emergency doors after a phone call getting clarification on the process of committing my seventeen-year-old child into the psychiatric ward for help with a mental breakdown and drug addiction. I explained to the receptionist that I didn't know what we were supposed to do as hot tears rolled down my face and my bottom lip quivered violently. Later I would learn that his violent behavior was a result of a nasty opioid detox process which wreaks havoc on a person's internal system.

And survivor's guilt.

I may never truly know what took place the night our entire lives changed course. Maybe, looking back, I don't need or want to.

The day was long and disturbing. I sat in a tiny blue suicide room with my son as he slept in a hospital gown. He was a 200 pound 6'2 man-child. He was frustrated.

We were both scared. But when he handed me his motorcycle rings with fright and anger in his eyes, all I could think of was I'd rather him be angry at me and alive, then dead. I imagined standing in the mortuary and someone handing me those rings and the image solidified we were at the right place for now. It was our new reality. He needed to be his own warrior now and I needed to be grateful for the reality of the moment.

You see, on December 28th, in the frigid early morning hours, four of my sons' friends attempted to wake a fifth boy who had overdosed on morphine and Xanax during recreational partying the night before. The reality of our world shifted very quickly.

On January 1st, I was admitting my son into the hospital as he was drowning in angst and grief.

On January 1st I was a blubbering, tired, starving, painful mess.

On January 1st around 2 am I had walked into my bathroom and literally flipped God off with both fingers high in the air as I was praying, cussing and yelling at him at the same time.

I asked him "what am I supposed to do now?". My cursing was out of control in the heated moment. How do we get past this?

When desperation kicks in it will bring you to your knees.

Today, God answered my cry. He answered the prayers I so desperately prayed yesterday. I needed my son to be able to mourn his friend after a short stay in a psychiatric treatment facility and He granted that. I asked Him for my son to keep his job and He granted that. He gave me the strength and dignity to be straight forward and hit this issue head on and I can feel His strength in this situation. I can hear Him whispering it has a purpose, but today, I just can't see what that purpose is.

I'm a day late as you can see. And to be honest if I told you that wouldn't happen throughout the rest of the journey recorded throughout these pages I would probably be sinfully lying. We have 5 kids, 3 dogs, a bird, a fish, and a daughter in law with our first grandchild growing in her belly. You'll get to know us all over the course of a year, and I hope, you can learn from whatever life lessons we go through. We are a real-life family. There is no keeping up with the Joneses. Honestly, I don't even think I know any Joneses.

I'm not sure if I can get through this entire journey, but I am willing to try it to strengthen my relationship with God for my children and my family.

This is my living journal and my living testimony.

Wednesday January 3rd, 2018

I picked up a book while Christmas shopping at Sam' Club.

Just this morning I was able to pick it up and catch up. Ironically it is a daily Guideposts publication. I'm three days behind. This book I've dedicated myself to for the year is a daunting task right now. I'm struggling to open-up emotionally. I've promised my brother I'd attend a church service with him. I need to own up to that. I'll send him a message tomorrow. I just don't think I am ready yet.

I need God right now. And I'm trying to find Him.

But when I read a couple of the scriptures this morning, they brought burning tears to my eyes. They were spot on. Through all my anger and through all my angst I find that a new strength was born this week. A strength for my marriage and family and a strength for my son. A new passion emerged from the depths of this tragedy we are facing.

I thought about them throughout my day as we had some hurdles with my son's medication and communication from the hospital. My ex-husband approved two different medications and did not call to discuss them with me. The nurse claimed to have tried to reach me and as it turned out they had written my number down incorrectly.

I addressed each concern with faith and a directness that I don't know if I've ever had in my life.

We had an amazing visit with our son tonight. I have a new-found respect and love for a seventeen-year-old kid who is really attempting to make the most out of his own convictions and tragedy.

I cannot lose faith in him, if I do, his faith will waiver and the tiny glimpse I saw in the remnants of his freckled face is just enough to keep me going.

__Now faith is the substance of the things hoped for, the evidence not seen. --Hebrews 11:1 (NKJV)__

Two nights ago, as I stood in my bathroom with my two middle fingers in the air, I wasn't prepared for God to give me the strength to do what I had to do, and yet He has.

__On the day I called you, You answered me; my strength of soul increased. --Psalm 138:3 (ESV)__

I called Him, and He answered. And He gave me a new passion. But I can't talk about it just yet. Tomorrow, maybe.

Wednesday, January 17th, 2018

This was supposed to be three hundred and sixty-five days with God. Turns out, I'm a lot worse at it then I previously thought. In my own defense I've got a lot on my plate. And I'm behind in a lot of other things too. My journal, my devotional...life...but, I've not stopped praying.

A lot has happened in the last month. I'll say that December was so full of emotions that I've almost felt hungover these last two weeks. Almost. We don't really have the luxury of just sitting and experiencing.

Let's start at the truth. Maybe it will make up for the daily lack of interest I seem to have in sharing my relationship with God.

Our son is only slowly getting better, but when I say slowly, I mean slowly. I am only slowly adjusting to a new way of life. I must adjust to the fact he was taking pills. Weed? That is the least of my worries. We must adjust to the raw truth of what our kids are faced with daily. The "good" kids, the "bad" kids...they're all fighting the same battle. But what I can't seem to understand is that some of the adults are just allowing it to happen.

It turns out the opiates that my sons friend had, they all had them. They were all taking them.

They also bought cocaine with their Christmas money. There was a three-day binge floating around social media and no one said a thing. Why? These kids are selling and taking medication like candy. The recreational partying, which is seemingly normal, is dark and twisted and tainted with depression and social anxiety. All kinds of kids are experimenting. In rural America it isn't just the "poor kids", but the bored kids, the sports kids, and the church kids. But it isn't just the teenagers. It's the parents too. Drugs are alluring and addictive. They make you feel good. Maybe the problem is that we are doing it to ourselves. We are literally driving ourselves to self-medicate with prescriptions and alcohol and illegal drugs. It's a slippery slope of adulthood that we don't want to talk about because then the blame lies on our shoulders. Parents across the nation are coming home from their day and struggling to stay sober to cope. That stress eats away at the common core of the otherwise healthy American family. It has spread like a disease. A night cap has turned into a lunch-cap to make it through the rest of our day. An occasional tension headache is now a deep rooted and over-medicated migraine along with a never-ending supply of pain pills. Drug dealers are no longer a scary pimp on the corner. They are in and on every corner of our kids' lives.

When I hugged Alex's mom at the funeral it was literally the heaviest my feet have ever been. I forced myself to do it. Not because of anything other than my out of control emotions and gratitude that my son was alive and hers was dead. As I sit here typing I can still feel her small body in my arms. And I can feel the pain in that statement. I know you can too.

I can't take it sometimes. And if I can't take it, how is my son supposed to? I can't do it alone, God. Do you hear me? I CAN'T DO IT ALONE. So, I pray, when I'm not too exhausted or wound up to remember. I pray for things like money to pay the medical bills rolling in. We currently have over $8,000 dollars' worth, that is with insurance. Could you imagine if we didn't have insurance? I pray for our vehicles to continue to run to get him back and forth to work and his counseling sessions. I pray for help and guidance and more strength because I don't really know how much I have left. I can't even drink a glass of wine without worrying about whether I'll have to leave to address something. I was diagnosed with severe anxiety disorder the day before this child died.

And I myself am taking a daily medication to cope with my nerves.

I am in the process of attempting to start a non-profit to introduce all the issues these kids and parents are facing to our local communities. Because I must do something. Maybe I can bridge the growing gap. Maybe I can make a difference. But I can't do it without God. I know that. I just don't know where to start.

Phone entry: February 23rd, 2018 - *"I heard a soft whisper of a voice today. God? The voice said, "a servant to my family and a servant to the Lord."*

Phone entry: March 4th, 2018 - *"I made a promise to Tosha that her sacrificial lamb would not die in vain. And I believe he is lying in the embrace.*

The rest of the pride, all of us, will avenge his name and we will step up and save the young people of our world.

If my voice cracks or wavers I apologize in advance. I've been emotional the last few months and passionate since Alex died, and a part of my son died with him. I'm not used to giving a speech or a talk, I'm a writer.

Look around you. We need to remove the invisible line that was set long ago between the good kids and the bad kids. We need to recognize that once we remove the barrier, and if we do, these kids can save each other. We need to stop putting them against each other. Educators, community leaders and parents are responsible for this epidemic.

I'm not perfect. The answer doesn't lie in perfection. Quite the opposite. It's the imperfections. That is where we are all at.

Everyone wants answers. But the answers are in our community. We need each other. Contrary to popular belief it does take a village to raise a child. We need that mentality back.

The social war on our teenagers needs to stop. Every day matters."

Throughout this book I will share with you some of my raw phone entries so you can see just where I was during our journey together. On a comical note, when I die, someone may think this poetic mama was cuh-razy.

Chapter One, Chapter One
The Start Over

The interesting thing about this book, was that I started it before salvation. Or so I thought. But God was speaking to me long before I dipped my body into the pool of warm water at our church.

Phone entry:

> *March 24th, 2018 I assumed the first time I gave my testimony would feel like what I imagine baby birds fledging from their nests feels like. Nervous but natural. I can only tell you that the time is here. And that I was moved to tears this evening thinking about how many times I've shown grace, even when told not to, and now many times the Lord has shown me and my children grace in the most trying of times.*

Day 279.

Monday October 8th, 2018

This.

This chapter is where it all changes.

You cannot go to the Father without going through His Son. Jesus Christ is and was the Savior and gift to us all. It isn't a "social" problem. It is a conviction problem. ***This*** is where it gets good.

Lpoo;k;opl;[(← cat feet typing welcome to my life)

The worry for a true born-again Christian for a non-Christian doesn't come from a place of vanity and judgement. It comes from a slightly selfish and heartfelt human place of fear that when we get to heaven, we won't see you again. I am biting back tears as I write that and I'm not sure why, I suppose because the truth rings so loud it can be deafening as I sit in service or pray for my family. You cannot go to Heaven unless you know Jesus Christ.

<u>**Day 279**</u>. How did I get to day two hundred and seventy-nine? I am much worse at this than I originally thought. Or so it seems.

I guess we start over from here. It's almost like a "Chapter One, Chapter One".

I read over my last entry. Our Pastor says you know you've been born again when your life has truly changed. He says everything about your life will change. Your friendships, your family relationships, your compassion, your willingness to serve a supernatural God, habits will change & even the way you love yourself changes. I believe he is right. As I look back over the last nine months since I started this project there are few things that are the same. But the core of who I am and what my heart looks and longs for has certainly changed.

I thought maybe it might be good to look at today's verse.

"Every good and perfect gift from above, coming down from the Father of heavenly lights, who does not change like shifting shadows." James 1:27 (NIV)

God gives us our gifts. When I started writing years ago, for an actual paycheck, I started in young adult paranormal fiction. Oh, you read that right. I then moved through a phase of writing romance. Then back to young adult fiction again. I loved the supernatural. I also loved to take real life circumstances and weave them into unbelievable fiction. It was cathartic. But it wasn't of God. Or for God.

Our story kind of turns into a workbook now. I encourage you to take notes, to write on the pages, and to scribble until your little heart is content. What a funny path I have taken thus far!

In Latin the meaning of the name *Tiffany* is: Manifestation of God.

No irony, that Alex, means "defender of mankind" and Tylor can mean "brick layer". My my, it seems names are important after all. Why is this important?

What is the meaning of your name?

The irony that my mother might have had some pre-destined reasoning for naming me Tiffany is both comical and ironic. Alex the defender and Tylor the brick layer paved the way to my salvation. I don't cite the meanings as a form of self-absorption. The irony should give you chills.

I cite the name definition because it's the first time in my life I am proud of my name as I proclaim God's love for me and the chosen people of the Kingdom. I cite the definition of the name because my book might be your manifestation of God and that is my best prayer. Because He can change your life so profoundly.

> *"There is therefore now no condemnation for those who are in Jesus Christ" Romans 8:1*

That is a big promise. But as of yesterday, it is a promise I can finally embrace and try to understand, but on a daily basis. I am so grateful for God's promise and truth in this verse.

When I run through my list of sins, before yesterday, I condemned myself daily for them. I couldn't understand that God's love for me was similar love as I have for my own children, but...better! Because His love is perfect. He doesn't run through my sins. He isn't the one reminding me of my sins. I do that. And Satan does. The enemy is the root of the attack on a family. There isn't any amount of social justice that can remove Satan from this earth.

Those who will condemn me even for writing this book will say "But she did _____" and "she said this!". The laundry list is there. Don't we all have a basket full of dirty laundry!

I was a good child. But I was a feral teenager.

The most disturbing part is that my teenage years were tame compared to some of the other teens I knew and interacted with, most were broken and yet some were middle class all-American kids who just made terrible choices. My decisions came partially because we grew up in poverty that was riddled with violent abuse of all kinds.

I scored a 10 on the coveted "ACE" test. The ACE test was invented as a way for us to gauge trauma. I would spend a better part of my twenties trying to outrun a past that just wouldn't go away. If it weren't for son "number one", I'm not sure where I might have ended up.

That boy changed my life. He was my very first gift from God.

I have peppered myself in the community here. I start most of my community speaking with, "I'm a terrible public speaker, but an expert on tragedy. For some of my fellow Missourians, you may remember in 1987 when Glen Paul Sweet shot highway patrolman Russell Harper. The day he shot Officer Harper, my step-father received a phone call and proceeded to inform us that Glen would be staying with us for a few days. I didn't understand the magnitude of the situation until later in my young adult life. Glen never showed up and we all know why, I can still take you to the house where he locked himself up in the attic and was shot out of. Had he been given the opportunity; a shootout might have taken place at our home."

Most my age or a little older nod their head in recognition. It was a dark day in our State's history.

But the man my stepfather was, wasn't any different than the violent criminal and heartless man that Sweet was. Oftentimes my step-father would lay in the yard in full camouflage in a drug induced haze and wait for police officers to show up. He took drugs. He was an cruel alcoholic. He beat my mother, brother, and I.

He sexually assaulted women. He brought perverted men around us. He had a nasty hatred for the law and anything involving it. He followed a cult religion. The list is really long.

He was the scariest man in my life. When he passed away was the only time, I've allowed myself to feel a disturbing gratitude for death. I wanted to see his casket be buried and I wanted to throw that first fistful of dirt. It was as Ecclesiastes says: "a time to die", and it was why I had wanted to kill him several times in my life.

It was the first time in my life I was able to recognize that the devil may have had a grip on his soul, and he will go straight to a burning eternity for the things he did.

If he chose God in the end, well, I just don't know that I believe a man like that would have. Our Pastor recently said, "God doesn't believe evil things that happen to you are good for you." I'm grateful for that statement. I just wish I had heard it a little earlier in life.

I can remember parking down the road from our old single wide trailer house in my early twenties. I smoked cigarettes until I had a belly-ache and finally made the decision that burning down the house with him in it wasn't the answer. But that fantasy was real for me.

If I told you the thought didn't run rampant throughout my adult life, I would be blatantly lying. If I told you I didn't drive by it over the next fifteen years and contemplate how I could do it and get away with it, I would be lying.

When I was a teenager, I often imagined myself shooting him to protect my family, and there were times in my adult life that I recognized I had an opportunity to kill him in self-defense and it would have been erased from my record at eighteen. I wanted to kill him. That is the human me. That is the reality of my past. The things that happened to my siblings and I in that house were the core of true evil and of Satan. There isn't any other explanation. I allow myself to feel what I feel, and I give it to God.

I don't think that is my biggest sin.

There was a heated and saucy affair between my marriages with a married man, a struggle with depression, I've divorced twice, I survived teenage promiscuity and a sexual assault when I put myself into a situation I should have avoided, a very short dance with alcohol my senior year of high school and moments where I turned to every type of god but the God of our universe. I stumbled through my thirties looking for love in all the wrong places. I blamed my first husbands' affairs on myself. I made excuses for my mean and sometimes intolerable comments to others on social media. I fell in with a crowd that had obvious disdain for all that is Christian and positive and cloaked it in a pagan message of self-love, when really it was self-destruction. At the end of the day, yoga and meditation left my soul empty. And it certainly wasn't curing anything.

My second divorce tore what little bit of compassion I had left, right out of my chest. Divorce and family betrayal will bring out the worst in a woman. When I suffered through this a second time, I wasn't sure I could recover. It's a rabbit hole of mental and emotional struggles. The judgement was damaging to my core.

I turned so far away from God that I'm not even sure how I arrived back here other than the fact that His love was so strong for me He didn't let go. I cried out "O God, please help me" through my second divorce when my family didn't support it. I have cried out to God after downing a bottle of wine and barfing in the neighbor's yard after watching my oldest son battle his own demons.

All the while my Father loved the human me so much that He continued to pull me through some of the most difficult times one can experience. He cried with me and for me. He cried out to me repeatedly. "I am" here, He responded when I asked where He was, and He shouted my name back at me.

He kept putting me back together again and again. And every time I was and am still human.

The lack of a Father can put a girl into precarious situations. Oftentimes she wades through life seeking the love of men and a world who over-sexualizes women. All the while the man she seeks is above her. He lies in wait. He comforts her spirit in her darkest times. Jesus Christ does not turn His face away from you, girls!

He is trying to hold it up. Just look at Him. Once you do, once you truly look at His face, you won't be able to ignore the sovereign grace that is rained down onto you. You won't need to seek your self-worth in sex, drugs or alcohol, possessions or worldly acceptance. Your relationship with God will change everything.

To be honest, I don't even know what my biggest sin is anymore. I've been studying the book of Romans.

> *"There is therefore now no condemnation for those who are in Christ Jesus". Rom 8:1*

No condemnation. **No condemnation.**

Let's go back to the beginning again. Because after "Chapter One, Chapter One", you might be wondering how I came to know and understand God's love for me and the collective "us". How did the story change so quickly?

Testimony is funny like that.

Chapter Two
Open House

<u>*Friday April 27th, 2018*</u>

It had been 4 months almost to the day that Alex died.

I started a non-profit in January of 2018 that geared towards helping families break the stigmas attached to mental illness battles and teenage drug use to wake up our community to a real-life monster lurking in the shadows waiting to devour our youth up one by one.

Friday was our ribbon cutting. How or why Mr. Morris (our state representative) was invited I can't recall. I may have been so bold as to invite him. I had no idea how the meeting would change my life forever. Mr. Morris and I had crossed paths the year before when my daughter had received state art honors in our capital city. That moment had been fleeting.

April 27th was not.

I was disappointed when he didn't show for the ribbon cutting. I was feeling frustrated because like most people, I was hoping the photo in the paper would help spotlight our organization and the mission we were on. I needed Mr. Morris' clout, selfishly. And we needed money to operate on.

At this point, Alex's death was even more difficult than in those first few weeks. I needed people to see Mr. Morris there and say "Wow! Look, this organization must be so important!"

I stumbled around in my high heels cleaning up the mess the open house had left behind. The door opened and the makeshift wind chime attached to the handle clacked loudly against the glass.

And there was Mr. Morris. Late. The photographer was gone. The reporter was gone. The other business owners were gone. Now what was I supposed to do?

Mr. Morris admitted he was avoiding the show.

I shuffled my way over to him and offered him a seat. My husband took the seat beside me.

What transpired from the moments following his arrival is the defining moment in my walk through the gates of Christianity.

Mr. Morris shared his testimony. It was a moving walk with God. He shared stories of his struggles with his blended family. He shared stories of his struggles with his teenagers. And he shared stories of his struggles with politics and public opinion, and most importantly, God.

I believe to this day the Holy Spirit was revealing Itself through Mr. Morris. I am a "people collector", I am deeply and profoundly moved by human interaction and this is how you can get my attention. I love collecting people. Here was one, I needed to listen to.

The most important part was his testimony regarding his walk with God and how humbled he is by the Lord and the miracles we are given if we dare to pay attention. My husband and I spent an emotional two hours with Mr. Morris and a friendship was born. Tears fell on both sides of the table.

Before he left, he told me he would love for us to attend church with him and his wife. I smiled and nodded my way through his invitation knowing I would probably shelf the invitation, and our moment would pass.

He was SO passionate and moved by his church's dedication to God. I was spiritually moved by his testimony. In my heart I feared the backlash and judgement that would come from everyone who knew the tougher version of me. I was fearful of giving up my freedom to sin. I was guilty of self judgement and societal judgement. I wanted to hide from God, still.

God had chosen me in my twenties during my dance with Mormonism, to teach the young adult's class and I had declined and never returned to church.

Besides, I didn't want God involved with our non-profit. As a matter of fact, I was dead set I didn't need God to solve this community problem. This wasn't a ministry.

I left that day exhausted and emotional, but I couldn't seem to shake the encounter.

God's pull through Mr. Morris' testimony didn't leave me. It rooted its way deep into my heart and it slowly released into my bloodstream over the course of a few days. It penetrated my soul. I finally messaged Mr. Morris on May 2nd and asked him where we could meet him to attend service.

I needed to see God one more time. I needed to give Him one more chance.

Sunday May 6th, 2018

Five months after I vowed to spend the year with God I was preparing to walk through the doors of a church. Obviously, I had spent more time trying to avoid Him, so I am sure he heard my battle cry from his throne. I mean you can just hear the humor in the testimony, the part where I denied needing His help, right?

He's funny like that.

The irony and humor in this part of the story might be how God brought me back to Him. I am forever humbled by His grace on my overall human temperament.

Our mega-church sits on a gorgeous piece of property facing the highway in our all-American city. It is a Pentecostal church. My first husband was Pentecostal, and I vowed to NEVER walk through the doors of a Pentecostal denominated church.

Never say never, right ladies?

Speaking in tongues was devilish and weird. They were judgmental and obnoxious. They hated everyone. And I was not going to wear my hair styled in a bun the rest of my life. And I am wearing pants.

Judge much? Turns out it isn't the denomination; it was the affect my first husband's interpretation had on me that caused me to avoid it like the plague.

And my own social ignorance.

I had vowed to NEVER attend such a massive church, well kind of, church in general. I am serious. I'm kind of embarrassed to say that out loud, to be honest. My husband probably chuckles at that now. He says he always knew I would fall in love with it. There were several reasons. I'll tell you about them, just so you can laugh at my vanity and judgement.

One, my husbands' ex-wife attends the church. Let's just say that the relationship there is a heated one, and one I continue to pray for daily. We tolerate one another for the sake of my beloved stepson.

Two, it is an over-sized, over-done, ostentatious place to worship the Lord. They probably wouldn't even let a homeless person in the front doors. Can you imagine the amount of self-indulged, self-absorbed, judgmental "Christians" who attend such a place? I mean come on; Jesus didn't worship in temples like this. "He" sat with the prostitutes and the homeless.

Three, they serve fancy coffee. How middle class is that? And they have a VIP for their youth center and loud music.

Self-absorbed-fancy-pants Christians.

Do you see where I am going with this?

The one decided factor for me in life for most things is human reaction, I've explained that already.

But one testimony is all it took.

We sauntered through the doors after checking our twelve-year-old son and sissy (our daughter) in at the VIP youth center, me, begrudgingly.

I knew I would hate going to this giant rich white person church. I mean to be fair it was the poor girl, raised on the rough side of town in me, coming out.

"Welcome Home". Door greeters. Smiling faces.

Original.

Not.

God doesn't want me. And sweet Jesus, oh sweet Jesus, what would He do with my children? How in the world can He heal my family? My pagan lifestyle and my disdain for all things conservative? I mean, I've been divorced. ***Twice***. Yeah right.

Sit down and smile Tiffany and just get through it. You're trying it right? And that gives me a logical and continuing argument as to why I don't embrace religion.

Here's what really happened.

I was intrigued with the welcoming atmosphere. No one really addressed Mr. Morris with the regular "Ooohhh". He was just another human. His wife was normal and real.

Most of what I explained on the page before this one, happened. Just differently than the atmosphere I previously set. Writers are funny like that.

The amazing thing was the moment the worship started the atmosphere changed immediately.

The congregation stood. Everyone sang in unison as the most beautiful voices echoed throughout the hall. A thousand people stood and worshipped together. Their arms were spread open wide up towards heaven and tears filled the eyes of our seat mates.

The Bible says,

"Is any among you sick? Let them call the elders of the church to pray over them and anoint them with the oil in the name of the Lord. And the prayer offered in faith will make the sick person well; the Lord will raise them up. If they have sinned they will be forgiven." James 5:14-15

One of the main singers speaks out into the crowd and he recites this verse. People move forward. I am immediately moved by a small family carrying their wheelchair bound son to the alter. The hot tears of my own humble emotion fill my soul. What a brat I could be.

The gospel starts to spread like some sort of wildfire and people around me are praying and speaking quietly in a heavenly language. Their voices are whispers and yet they are so loud even through the music I hear them buzz.

The praying! Oh, how beautiful the praying was to hear that morning.

By the end of the Pastor's message I find myself crying out inside to the Lord. I need Jesus.

I know He is moving me forward in my spirit. I am begging Him to take away our pain and our stress and to save my son.

I need Him to save our family from the tight grasp of the devil. "I will give you my children", I silently cry out to Him. I raise my hand to go forward. I don't think anyone sees me because many have their heads bent in prayer.

That's what I thought.

Then he asks for us to come forward. In front of a thousand people and proclaim we are giving our life to the Father and the Son.

My feet are like cement bricks. My knees are wobbly. I feel a tap on my shoulder and the lady behind me offers to go with me. I accept. We are walking, I am almost floating down the aisle with me wiping my blubbering face and shaking, I allow several people to put their hands on me and pray. They're crying, I'm crying.

The small room we are led to is filled with some members waiting to pray with me and give me a Bible. I struggle with this because somewhere, I have a Bible. And a book of Mormon. I tell them I am a recovering Mormon. Where are my books at? I struggle to remember. I think they are in the trunk by my front door. It's filled with the kids' baby books and photo albums and strategically placed so in a disaster I can drag it out of our front door.

I take the gift anyways and accept the prayers graciously. The irony is that later, when we arrive home, I wasn't able to find either one of those books.

The children are waiting for us in the youth center. They ask what took so long, I explain I was moved by the Lord and we will be attending church again.

I understand later after reflection, that God has literally moved forward in social time to keep up and continue to transform modern lives. He has moved forward. He recognizes his people and how fast they are developing and moving. Wow! This is what the modern-day Jesus culture looks like.

On Sunday, May 20th, when Mike and I make our way over to the youth center to retrieve the "littles" as we refer to them, they aren't there. A young girl tells us they have decided to give their life to the Lord and are receiving their Bibles. It's not a perfect gift as I later learn when sissy struggles to get baptized, but a gift nonetheless and the Spirit moved them to do so. Their salvation is now in God's hands. To be honest I felt an odd sense of relief.

I owe Mr. Morris and a seventeen-year-old boy who over-dosed and died credit for my salvation. I know those words are harshly received, people don't like it when others use the word, died. But they ring true. That is the gift that Alex's death by overdose was, it is what he left here for me. His death might be the saving grace in many lives to come. Mr. Morris should know his testimony saved an entire family from the wrath of God and hell itself. It's cosmically important for people to see the power of a true testimony and the rawness associated with it.

Because as we move forward in the story you will begin to see the beginning, and the power, of God's grace in our life.

Do you understand grace?

_____
_____
_____

Chapter Three
Phoebe

Sometimes a writer has a style. I've learned over the years that I have a faster pace than some. I accepted the difference of my style a while back. As we bob and weave forward through each chapter we will explore some of the days spent in church or prayer meeting. Some days I will tie these days to events that unfold as the year goes by, my prayer for you is that you are able to cognitively move through my style and not judge me for my quick and often-times humorous approach to life itself.

While we move through instances and scripture, what do you feel your gift from God is?

_____
_____
_____
_____
_____
_____

<u>**Sunday May 13th, 2018**</u>

Happy Mother's Day!

If I told you that up until this day, this year, my walk with God was easy I would be lying. He kind of shoved me kicking and screaming like a good Father would do. It took me a few years to adjust to the relationship I had with my own father, who spent most of my life, absent. When I was a little girl, after my step-dad had beaten one of us, I would lay in bed and pray for my father to rescue me. My biological father.

I would pray to my Father for my father to rescue me.

Boy, how strong are those words? Fortunately for me my Father knew my heart. God was already planning to rescue me. I don't hate my father now, but the relationship is forever defined by our past. You don't get over pain, you simply get through it. Even as a young girl I believed in God and I believe He listened to me, even if I were angry with Him. There were nights I would cry out to Him, how could He let some of the things that had happened to me, happen? How? Why?

Later as an angry teenage girl, I hated Him.

I hated that He didn't love me enough to take me out of the situation, now I realize my God was helping me through the situation.

He was listening.

But when we chose humanity, we chose free will, and some miracles are not in the cards because the lesson and experience help us later. Our trials and tribulations are what define our testimony. There is no perfection in a testimony. Could you imagine if every single time someone spoke of their testimony it was only "perfect" and without the "ugliness" of humankind and our sins?

Mother's Day of this year was one of those days where I realized that not only was I not longing for my mother's love and affection anymore, but not my father's as well. I was after my Father's heart.

Our Pastor's wife gave the sermon. It wasn't until later that I realized she was also a Pastor.

The sermon was about Phoebe. Phoebe opened up a world of the girls in the Bible like nothing else had before. Before I was a Christian, I had assumed the women in the Bible were holy and righteous, something I could never seem to be.

I couldn't get enough of Phoebe and that sermon. How Paul loved her so as a sister in Christ? She had become the messenger for the most important story in the world.

And Phoebe was a slave girl.

More than likely she was abused and exploited in more ways than one. She was broken and bruised and yet she radiated in the love of Christ.

Phoebes love and devotion to her Father put her on a path to walk one of the very first walks for women today. She was an early messenger of God.

In days when women were treated with little or no respect, Christ gave her respect and love.

The following are from my notes from our Mother's Day lesson:

1. Our past should not determine our future – The truth to this should ring true no matter what stage of your life you are in. We know from evolving experience that moving forward, your past may influence your future, but it does not dictate it, especially when you are in Christ. Christ gives us a pardon. It is a pardon from the highest judge from the highest court in existence. Truth be told, all we must do is accept His perfect love and with the flick of a finger we are forgiven, we simply must ask. He doesn't erase our memory, but He gives us the strength to see it, embrace the emotion, and then to move

forward and let it go. It is our human nature to let it stubbornly hang around. In our life, just because my son made a mistake doesn't deem him a mistake in God's eyes. God sees past our sin. God knows our sin. God knows our struggle because He always goes before us. Christ goes on to name other women in Romans 16. This is important for the women of Christ, especially now, when so many women are turning away from Christs perfect love. Today's feminist movement is not of Christ. Christs order for the world is Christ, man, woman, children. Women are not disposable. They weren't then, and they aren't now. Paul shows us how important Phoebe was in the early days of Christ and the church.

"For when you were slaves of sin, you were free regarding righteousness. But what fruit were you getting at the time from the things of which you are now ashamed? For the end of those things is death. But now you have been set free from sin and have become slaves of God, the fruit you get leads to sanctification and its end, eternal life." Rom. 6:20-24

2. NEVER GET YOUR WORTH FROM OTHERS – *Psalm 18:3 "I call upon the Lord, who is worthy to be praised, and I am saved from my enemies."* Amen to that. As a mother of 2 teenagers that used drugs, living a middle-class life, in a conservative fly over state, I'm speaking to the women struggling with this statement. Break it down, sister. Once you are in Christ, you are in Christ. I know you may struggle with that conclusion and still bite back at your own demons because we have been raised to be strong, independent and fierce women. But let me tell you something, if the thought of crossing over into Heaven without the ones we have loved on Earth isn't a helpful force in your salvation, eternal life with not only our

creator, but those with whom he created us with, then I just don't know what is. Those of us who have lost someone to an addiction or an overdose struggle with these things. We truly must reach down deep to muster up the words "I don't care what _____ thinks" as we look away and fight back hot tears. The isolation of unexplained human choice (free will) and tragedy says otherwise. Friends stop calling. "Real life Christians" stop calling. Your world just changes. It becomes difficult to come to terms with those who are hindering your spiritual growth and who is not. The ones left standing after you have received Christ are the ones you can move forward with. Choosing a life with Christ is easy. The aftermath of human nature is not. But when your heart changes and the eternal love of our Lord and Savior is what you start to seek you will experience relief and an outpouring of "me too's", more than you realize. They mean something.

God will cloak you in love and righteousness. He will show you and guide you forward.

3. Use your position in life right at this moment – I had a hard time with this. There's a story behind it, that if I don't share, it won't show you how much I related to this. Alex's mom and I have become close since Alex died. Not only do I have an eternal obligation to help her keep hold of the rod, I have an eternal obligation to show her that I appreciate the sacrifice she has made. I realize that Alex has now become my poster child for not turning away from teenagers struggling with addiction and mental illness or crisis in general. A couple of months ago we had an event at a local collegiate ballpark. Our goal is always to inform parents of the things are kids are in danger of. We pass out literature, there is a picture

of Alex, and I tell our story to anyone who I can get to listen. Tosha began to tell me a story of a lady we both have known a very long time. The story started out with a "Now don't get upset" ... (you can practically feel my cheeks flushing now). No woman likes a story to start out in this way. "So and so sent me a message and told me she was afraid you were going to use Alex to make money and for fame". Cut frame, pan to my red, angry, face full of hot tears.

I was hurt and I was so angry. Why? Because our platform is how we keep other kids from dying. Because spending months hounding and checking on my son to make sure he had not killed himself had taken its toll on me. I had spent months on my knees and at a child's grave...alone, scared, and angry. I don't want another mother to experience what we have experienced. Not because it isn't fair, but because it is painful. It has been so painful and so excruciating, that there have been moments when I thought I couldn't even get out of bed. The ache in my heart has seeped into my bones. My platform IS Alex's platform, and more importantly it is God's platform. I must use that platform to fund the word of God and arm families with the ability to treat addiction and mental illness in families. Our platform is important because it could save a child's life. Our platform is important because no family can get sober without the help and grace of God.

I struggled with that conversation for weeks.

Listen to me, woman of God. He chose you. You are a sister in Christ. Whether you are a recovering addict yourself, whether you are a mother, sister, or friend of someone struggling, whether you are single or married, He chose you. You use your platform to bring more people home to the kingdom. Everyone wants to watch science fiction. We want to pretend we are fighting a battle. Let me tell you something, you are in a live action fight between good and evil, and it's time to pick a platform and pick your side.

4. YOU NEED COURAGE. This statement was going to be important. SO important.

On August 19th, 2018, the day before my 40th birthday, sissy (our daughter) and I were scheduled to be baptized after service. I wouldn't know how Phoebe's lessons would come into play and how important that last one was until this day. Sis was struggling with her choice to become a Christian. You and I know the holy spirit moved her, but she is only eleven. She didn't want to get baptized.

She was ready to walk out and to be honest my own anxiety was about to let her. This was the first time I heard God command me in my everyday life. *"Go with her into the water, go before her as I have gone before you".* That was the defining moment. The moment I told her I would face the people with her was her defining moment she chose to be baptized by water. We linked arms that day and went under together. Give God an inch of your trust and he will give you a mile of courage.

"as it is my eager expectation and hope that I will not be at all ashamed, but that with full courage now as always Christ will be honored in my body, whether by life or by death." Phil 1:20

Don't be ashamed to love your heavenly Father. If you seek Him with your heart, He will reveal Himself to you and the courage will come along with perfect love.

I take notes in almost every sermon I attend. Sometimes you will see me refer to them as lessons. I would encourage this practice for you too. It really does help when you go home to study God's word for you. This is the academic in me who has a hard time separating the spiritual aspect from the eagerness to learn all things Godly and historically accurate. Between taking notes and digital access to sermons, you can literally have access to God's word at any point in your day. If you aren't toting your Bible with you.

Instagram.

Social media. It's how we reach the masses, right?

Don't we all have a love and hate relationship with this aspect of our technology ridden life. This is one of my Instagram posts:

<u>Sunday May 20th, 2018</u>

"Our Sunday story,

When we went to get the kids from youth services today, they were not in their usual spot.

They had decided to get saved. Together.

Now here's the deal, I made them commit to at least 4 Sundays. Now they've committed to an entire summer.

They don't fully understand their new commitment but felt compelled to go up front, in front of their peers and choose to be a Christian.

Erica said, "I raised my hand because Kyle raised his", and so they will learn God together. Probably bickering the entire time like the assumed twins people think they are. But they were moved by the spirit.

My Kyle. My scientist is going to examine and investigate his faith. He went first.

And the thing is, the details will fill themselves in as they learn to walk with God. And most importantly it's never too late.

Happy Sunday! I'm just proud and content with all our kids. They're making their own ways and putting forth effort to learn from mistakes and be good humans.

Sometimes in the darkest hours, something beautiful can come out of it and I won't take anything for granted. I am forever humbled by God's grace."

This Sunday's notes are almost chilling. Little did I know that the synchronicity in our lessons and the notes I would take over the next few months would show God's hands in both our sermons and the children's. I can't tell you anything spectacular about the weather or what we were wearing. But I can tell you the date is almost more important than my own salvation. Because this was the day that my children's salvation was given to the hand of God Himself.

No longer did I feel the burden of introducing God into their life because He showed Himself to them. Even if fleeting, because of their young age, His presence will now always be in their life because they chose to step forward and receive Christ.

For some of you who know our twelve-year-old son, you know how shocking it was to find out he was the one who led his sister to the front of the service.

My Kyle is an apparent shepherd.

Around this time our Pastor had started a series call "Get Smart- Get Wisdom".

James 1:5 says, "If any of you lacks wisdom, let him ask God, who gives generously to all without reproach, and it will be given him".

This series launched a new love for Christ in me and a thirst for knowledge like never before. I had so many questions and He had promised to answer them all.

I wrote in my notebook, "A child's salvation is in her parent's hands. We say that we don't want to force religion, but if we don't take them to church then we have chosen for them. If introduction to God never happens then we rob them of free will and a choice."

I sit here typing those words and know they ring true.

For me. For you. And for your family.

I renounced God for several years. Partly because I wanted to do what I wanted to do. How could someone know me, or my children better than I did?

But He does. God knows our children because He knew them before He created them. It took me a long time to tie this into my belief on abortion.

I will preface that statement with, I've known a lot of women who have had an abortion, I do not believe their sin is greater than mine. If you are my friend, know that I do not judge your choice. But I do believe now that showing a young woman, she is killing her own child, and God's child, is an atrocity. This all ties into the fact that if God knows our children, better and even before we do, how sad must He be when they die. If we do not give our children the knowledge to make an informed choice about God, then their salvation is on our hands as parents.

I didn't want that responsibility anymore. I wanted God to take this from my hands.

Let me explain that. Some of you right now, think that to be a selfish statement.

Matthew 19:13-14

"Then some children were brought to Him so that he may lay His hands on them and pray; and the disciples rebuked them. But Jesus said, Let the children alone and do not hinder them from coming to me: for the kingdom of heaven belongs to such as these."

We focus so much nowadays on children and their cognitive development that we often forget how important a healthy spiritual balance is. We choose to turn away from God, therefore making a choice for our children.

It isn't fair to allow a child to choose atheism if they do not truly understand what they are choosing.

If you give a child the choice, and you give them the knowledge they need, they will make a choice to follow God.

It may be a longer decision process for them, but one of the key factors in a relationship is consistency and trust. How can you expect a child to form a bond with God if you are the one standing in the way?

How can you as a mom open your child's world to God with a gentle hand?

_____
_____
_____
_____
_____
_____

I had, up until that point, been the one responsible for my children's salvation. It was selfish and cruel to keep them out of the house of God for my own reasons and sins. I wanted my children to be "spiritual" without having a relationship with the God who created them. That is *my sin*.

If nothing else, can I encourage you to evaluate your relationship with God and your own salvation? _____

When God says to give Him our troubles, He truly means it, and the freedom from doing so healed my anxiety in that regard. I have given my children to God. They are now in His hands. Introduce your child to God. Give them over to Him and allow His love to penetrate their lives, even if they are in turmoil.

Chapter Four
Kyle and the Church Bully

Proverbs 13:20

"Whoever walks with the wise becomes wise, but the companion of fools will suffer harm."

The Get Smart series really provoked a deep spiritual movement in me. I spent days listening to podcasts and evenings listening to gospel music. I started watching my sailor's mouth and using a softer approach with those around me. My life was transforming. At the time I didn't think much of it. I was in my cocoon of transformation I suppose.

When I look at the notes in my phone from June, the first entry is unsettling.

Sunday June 3rd, 2018

"Today Kyle really had a hard time with church. Finally got him around and made it early. He said he hates church. Was at his dad's last week and missed. I took the kids spirituality for granted. I left it on the shoulders of someone else. No more."

Later we would find out that Kyle was having a hard time with a church bully.

Yes, humans still behave human in Sunday services.

Evil can penetrate a heart, even under the rooftop of God's house, the enemy was pulling at my child's salvation and will to go to church.

Being a baby Christian, I hadn't prepared myself for this. As a matter of fact, I had no idea how to handle it, short of telling my son to punch this kid in the nose if he didn't leave him alone. Because it was constant!

Pastor's message that day was about safeguarding your heart. I can see the connection looking back now. He pointed out that the Bible mentions the words "The Heart" 601 times. I've lived most of my life by my heart. I guess it's important after all. And it is important for the parent too. But it is equally important to realize that it can be wicked.

We must apply the lessons in the Bible accordingly. They are written in a context that can be dissected today and applied to modern families. In our case, the bully, was the enemy's way of affecting Kyle's heart. A brand-new baby Christian heart. The heart was an easy target for our son.

> ***Proverbs 4:23 says, "Keep your heart with all vigilance, for from it flow the springs of life."***

Even when you're dealing with a bully. In church.

One of the hardest things I've had to do is lead by example by attending regular service.

But Kyle can't drive. And Kyle will face these situations his entire life if he is walking with Christ. And while we can't protect them from all things, including kid bullies, we can certainly arm them with God's armor.

Our son still struggles everyday with his Christianity. He is only a teenager. If I told you he didn't I would be misleading you into thinking we were transformed into a perfect family with a perfect life, and as you read on, you will realize that is most certainly not the case. And thank goodness our God is patient. Because Kyle's salvation is in the earliest stages. I can only encourage him to continue his walk with Christ. God will work daily in our boys' heart.

One thing we have learned over the course of the year, since Alex died, is that our youth are living in a very different world.

When I struggled with the devils attempts at my family, I started listening to podcasts and sermons about demons and the way the devil operates. What my research led me to was astounding.

The devil is real folks. Like, totally, unequivocally, one hundred and one percent, real.

On July 16th, 2018, this was my Instagram entry:

"What if it's all true?

What if there is an enemy out there and every day is a battle? A spiritual battle that makes the LOTR, for you pop culture fans, seem more true and even more real? I used to believe I was outnumbered by Christians. Now I believe I am outnumbered by those who choose to be unbelievers. Christians are the minority. And to some of you, I am sorry if I was disrespectful to your beliefs and values.

My journey with God started a long time ago. Then I skated off the path. I was angry. I was sad. I was so lost. He asked me to serve during my jaded dance with Mormonism and I ran like hell.

And he still loved me.

He loved me enough to keep trying. He sat still and allowed me to proclaim I was only spiritual, not religious. All the while probably smiling. Because he already knew me, and my children.

Then he sent me Mike. A man who's not only loved me, but 4 children he didn't biologically father, fiercely I might add, and then another 2 more teenagers. Kelsey and William. For those of you who don't know, William is my ex-husbands stepson. Mike attends service and he worships with me and he is the best example of a father and man that I've known, next to my Uncle Rick.

He's my world. And our family is everything.

Most of all the credit for my salvation belongs to Alex.

The boy who brought not just me, but slowly my family, to God, and is still working through Christ in us.

I've invited some of you to go to the Designed Sisterhood Night with me and I hope you do. If I tagged you, this is another invitation.

I guess every day I see the importance of the transformation that a relationship with God gives you. I'm still the same crazy and funny me, I'm just cussing less and focused on my connection with the supernatural God who loves us. I'm a BETTER me.

And if it's all true, I just want to meet you all in heaven. What a shame it would be to miss each other!

Please let me know if you can make it, we will need to be early to secure a seat. and there will be food, music and much more!"

The devil is very real. The battle between good and evil exists on Earth. We are living in the last days. As the sexual pressure surmounts among teenagers, as the pressure to fit in and succumb to ridiculous standards weighs down, as logic outweighs a spiritual connection with God, these teenagers are treading water and they are tired.

It is dark water. The devil knows that the way to crush a society is through the youth. If we allow the devil to enter our teenagers' hearts, and then to reside there, it will be a costly mistake. The devil is heroin. The devil is unprotected sex. The devil is absent parents and parents chasing material objects. The devil is a sensational and mutilating entertainment industry. It's everything our society is right now.

You don't have to take everything away from them but simply guide them to a gentler choice and spirit.

Better yet, let God have them.

On July 18th, I marked a page in my Bible. I marked it with 365 Days with God at the top of page 1,253. Today, when searching for my verses to include in this chapter, I realize now that I was prophetically marking what I would need later.

Ephesians 4:27 says, "and give no opportunity to the devil".

In Ephesians Paul talks about his time in prison. Paul understood that the devil has no boundaries when he descends on a child of God. The moment a household chooses to follow Christ, when the head of said household stands up and leads their family to Christ Jesus, they are now in the devil's bullseye.

Give no opportunity to the devil. That is a statement that should send a chill through your body. When you start viewing the world as a real-life battle between good and evil, where do you want your family to be at the end of the day? That was hard for me to come to terms with. Even though I had written supernatural fiction, I couldn't wrap my brain around it. But when you do arm yourself with the word of God, you can beat the devil.

Jesus Christ, the son of the God of our universe literally hands us the armor OF God.

We are then given the choice to put it on and BE a new person, a new warrior, reborn into a life of sovereign grace. Salvation is the key to the Kingdom. Quite frankly, that's where I want to end up.

Let that sink in folks. It's like a real life supernatural sci-fi. Like, full circle, I'm still writing supernatural. Only I am now living it too! See what God did there?

Chapter Five
God's "Will"

Four was a chapter about kids.

Five begins the ground altering argument that I continued to have with God over the next few months. And involves, yes, another kid.

My notes in my book get kind of sketchy and blank during this phase in my journey. And to be honest, I can't remember why.

But raise the red curtain and cue William.

God's Will.

My relationship with my first ex-husband and his wife has always been rocky. I can pretend it has not. I can lie and tell you that we've tried to love each other, but the truth of the matter is we haven't. We are not the picture-perfect fake family that embraced separation or trials. Our relationship has fallen short of the ever-popular fake divorced family you witness on social media spending the holidays together for, "the kid's sake".

There was hatred and betrayal and deeply rooted pain.

I used to be ashamed of it. I used to blame myself for his infidelity. I took all the brunt of the marriage failing and allowed myself to be manipulated.

When I say those things, they are unintentionally harmful. But I spent many years making excuses for behavior I should have never allowed. And some of that behavior and my inability to stand up for myself allowed both of my boys to experience pain and later, stumbles with substance abuse. Human dynamics are riddled with guilt, dysfunction, and self-destructive tendencies. This is precisely why we need our Lord and Savior.

Around June 20th Tylor called and asked me one of the hardest things he had no doubt planned on asking his mother.

The call went something along the lines of,

"Hey, I have a question" His deep voice always vibrates the cell phone speaker.

"What's that son?" I ask.

"Williams dad kicked him out and he doesn't have a place to go, would it be alright if he stayed with us for a while?" he asks. Silence.

Double silence. The silence is so thick you could cut it with a knife.

Really, Lord? *This* is what you are asking me to do. I can feel the tug on my already bruised heart.

William is my ex-husbands wife's son. Boy, that is a mouthful.

You can almost hear the humor in heaven at this point. The angels must have been waiting so quietly for my response you could have heard a proverbial heavenly pin drop.

And I don't mean that in a blasphemous manner.

"Let me call your bonus dad, I'll call you back." I tell him and then hang up.

The phone call between my husband and I was a basic repeat of the conversation between Tylor and I, and a whole 'lotta heavy silence. Mostly because my husband loves me so much and really struggles to tell me no. Also, he's one of the best humans I have ever had the privilege of doing life with.

"Husband?" I quietly ask.

"Yes, wife?" his voice on the other end is also quiet.

"Just making sure you didn't hang up on me." I say.

I can feel his broken heart and I can sense the stress in his voice. But let me tell you something about my husband. In our story, he is one of the most important characters.

He is directly below God.

> God.
>
> Husband.
>
> Wife.
>
> Children.

For the first time in my ever controlling, feminine existence, I let my husband have control, under my Savior. It's something that just works for us. Our blessings have been many, and our trials have been many. My husband is an absolute man of God. He has a hard time admitting it, he is working on his own salvation, but when I tell you that he is one of the kindest, smartest, and most compassionate men I've ever known, those are not strong enough words to describe him. I have no doubt that God will give him a reciprocating "Browning" hug.

"Whatever you think we need to do, wife." He says quietly.

We both know what that means. It doesn't mean the couple of days my son has asked for; it means until we have done what we can do for another kid.

What I can tell you about that day is embarrassing and painful. I didn't want to take him in.

Not because of a personal vendetta, but because I was exhausted. I wouldn't want him to read this and think otherwise. I was so tired of being tired that I wasn't even sure I could cope with the drama associated with the choice to let him stay. My pain was so bad at this moment that I didn't want to fail him.

I was physically, mentally, and emotionally exhausted. Since Alex's death I spent every day worrying about which one of my sons' friends would be next and intermingling that with my own sons struggle with suicidal thoughts and survivors' guilt. I didn't understand how my situation was helpful to yet another mouth to feed, another body to clothe, and another soul to align to God's plans. I cried in my car. I cussed at my Father. I cried again and then called Tylor to lay out the rules.

Galatians 6:2 says, "Bear one another's burdens and so fulfill the law of Christ."

Sunday, June 24th, 2018

William attended service for the first time. I felt a sense of peace. We had an open conversation regarding some past transgressions the adults had to work through, and although I know William struggles with the truth, he was ready to commit to a clean lifestyle. At least I believed he was.

Throughout the month of June William attended church with us. I truly believed the messages were reaching him, but each time he rebuked them. I'll tell you that his heart softened. I believe God touched him. I believe he will choose God, I just can't tell you when.

Sunday July 1st, 2018

I have written down,

Matthew 4:19, "And he said to them, Follow me and I will make you fishers of men".

This verse rings true for most of my month of July because as the Lord filled my heart, I began asking friends and family to church. That was way out of my norm.

The month of July proved to be an eventful one as Kyle chose to be baptized at church camp as well. But it was also full of trials at every single turn of the way.

We spent our Sundays at church, and I spent my Wednesdays at prayer meeting. I found that I couldn't get enough of the word of God. The spirit was so deep rooted in my heart that there was no denying Christ.

The issues at home were not easing up but we were bobbing and weaving like champs. The notes in my phone reflect how stressful the time was. And yet I was covered in God.

Phone entry: "July 8th. Missed church. Angry. Sad. Felt abandoned. Frustrated with God. Trying to get over this hump."

Phone entry: "July 22nd Judas? Argued with Mike and Gavin over the parental issues hangin' around after the pool party and *weird girl. Realized I was still hurt by his mother's betrayal. Tired. Bummed. Empty. But still hopeful. Just trying to get back to who I am. Not sure anymore."*

At the end of the month my first-born grandson made his way to Missouri. Tylor's demons were gaining strength again and we were watching him spiral out of emotional control. William was battling his own constant truth. We were gearing up for the Daniel fast and I was stumbling through my Christianity like a wobbly sailor after months at sea.

I was a train wreck. And yet somehow, I managed to fill up an entire row of seats with women to hear Lisa Harper bear her testimony. All I wanted to do was bring the women in my life to church with me. I needed them to hear God's word. The intense feeling of needing them in heaven with me was over-whelming.

As I prepared for my very first fast, I did the best I could to fit into a new church and try and make it shrink a little bit. But those first few months, man, they were really difficult for a new Christian girl.

Chapter Six
Daniel Fast-21 Days of Prayer

<u>Sunday July 29th 2018</u>

July 29th marked the beginning of the Daniel fast.

I didn't understand it. But I wanted to do it.

I failed miserably the first week. I struggled with blood sugar issues, I struggled with sleeplessness, I struggled in my faith. Boy was I cranky and hateful!

In my notes I have *Ephesians 3:14-16* wrote down.

"For this reason, I bow my knees before the father, from whom every family in heaven and on earth is named, that according to the riches of his glory he may grant you to be strengthened with power through his spirit in your inner being."

This time in my journey is important because it marks the beginning of my relationship with the Holy Spirit. Yes, **THE Holy Spirit**. I feel like you heard some sort of dramatic music just then.

Pastor must have said, "Prayer is the posture of the heart".

It's in the ink in my notes and it is the truth. You can start to feel your heart holding itself up when you grow stronger in prayer. Kneel, build your relationship with the Father, and pay attention to resource. The Holy Spirit will fill your body when you give your body to the Holy Spirit. When you pray, speak to your Father, address Him as Father. Cry out to Him with Father!

Paul is so passionate in his delivery and he is so passionate when he tells us that he was *"the very least of all the saints," Ephesians 3:8*. If that doesn't drive you, I don't know what will to be honest. If you don't know Paul's story, I would encourage you to read about Paul and his walk with Jesus Christ and his love for the gospel of all of creation. He uses his "platform" and he used it well. He uses his situation, not to blame God, but to recognize his own human weakness, and the strength of love and commitment to his Father and the Son. He uses his weaknesses to glorify our God.

The focus on *prayer* wasn't too difficult for me. Even in my most difficult times in my life, I prayed. Although I didn't cry out to Him by name all the times I prayed, I know He was still listening. This fast was difficult for me because it caused me to consider whether I was praying the "right" or "wrong" way. It wasn't until my fast that I fully recognized the importance of, "the only way to the Father is through the Son." I had been praying for years, but never in Jesus' name.

The first week was a disaster. I think in the end I probably consumed twice the number of calories in my feeble human existence. How in the world did Daniel do it?

Are you familiar to the Daniel fast or fasting in faith in general?

_____
_____
_____
_____

The second week my focus became more intense. My notes are furious in my book. The first week of August my brother and mother ran into family issues, they later recovered. I missed church. My first-born son and his wife were home and I was struggling with him leaving once again. And we were contemplating sending Tylor back to Washington with Lucas, our oldest son. On August 1st, my entry to my church journal reads, "so tired today and this week, but hopeful". I had been searching out the Judas in my life and was trying desperately to kindly and gracefully make some life changes.

I have John 14:21, *"Whoever has my commandments and keeps them, he it is who loves me. And he who loves me will be loved by my Father, and I will love him and manifest myself to him."* written down. I needed to be deeply rooted in love in order to be grounded in love. And I was treading water.

By the third week of fasting I finally convinced myself that I could do it. In my notes, I have a question written down, **"Do you know Christ as a person?"**. That was my kicker. I didn't. And I needed too. I needed to see Him in me, and myself in Him. This entire time I was hiding behind the fact that Christ wasn't human, when in fact, there was a short period of time He was.

And if God could give His only son, I could most certainly go without the human cravings for a few days.

I fasted at first with liquids. The last eight or nine days of the fast I alternated fasting my two meals a day and only eating after 8 pm and I gave up things like coffee. I was tired, wired, and some days crabby.

But I was patient. And I prayed. I begged the Lord to make Himself known to me. God uses power in His love.

The Bible uses the phrase "Do not be afraid, 365 times". One time for every single day of your year. During my fast I can tell you that

I was very afraid. I was afraid the Lord would not reveal Himself to me. I was afraid that God had forsaken me and somehow "tricked me into church". I was struggling with the boys and their decisions. I was struggling with my oldest son leaving again with my grandson. I needed for Tylor to agree to go back to Washington with his brother to get away from it all.

Part of that decision was a deep need to simply rest. To the mom reading this right now, I know you are struggling. I know you are quietly hoping you get rest. Rest from the addiction, rest from the mental illness struggle and rest from the stigma attached to parenting teenagers who go through a crisis. To the mom raising children on her own or in a home that is struggling right now, girl, boy do I know how you need physical and human rest. It is coming to you through Him.

On August 3rd my relief came. Tylor had agreed to an undecided number of days back in Washington. I needed those weeks that followed for sleep. I needed a chanced to rest and come to terms to where we were at and where we were struggling.

I needed to separate Tylor and William and give them some space to become their own person. They were still using. They were still partying. And Tylor was struggling with his place since Alex had died.

Sunday August 12th, 2018

In the months after Alex's' death and Tylor's hap-hazard recovery, we had started a non-profit to help families who had teens in crisis, I had reorganized my personal and social life, found God, argued with God, and opened a business to support the said non-profit. This was the beginning of the book and you saw how quickly God changed the course of our lives. But during my journey with salvation, the non-profit was trying to function but slowly, and it had eaten me alive whole-heartedly. I was living in a place of death.

When God wanted me to live in a place of life. His everlasting life. For He knows our difficulties and that is why we reach out to Him in fasting and prayer.

During our fast we were given a list of 7 reasons that fasting is so important. I can tell you that in each sentence came a sense of enrichment and holy grace as I realized that I was able to make it through the fast. Even as a baby Christian, my feeble attempt at fasting was better than giving God nothing at all.

My notes from August 12th say this,

> *"Week prior-bought book "7", started to understand the commercialization and all of our stuff. Focus on spirituality and experience instead. Rich vs. rich. Thought about missionary work."*

Boy howdy. Missionary work? Tiffany, are you kidding me? Do you know how many times I have said that I would never wave a Bible in front of another person's face in exchange for rice?

It's not about that though. As I starting to realize, ministry is about saving those who belong in the Kingdom and to God. It is about spiritual enlightenment. It's about a relationship with our Creator. It's about science, and math, and how it all fits together. The Bible is the be all and end all. It has the questions and it holds the answers.

Isiah 58:8-9 "Then shall your light break forth like the dawn, and your healing shall spring up speedily; your righteousness

shall go before you; the glory of the Lord shall be your rear guard. Then you shall call, and the Lord shall answer; you shall cry, and he will say, HERE I AM."

God hears our cries.

Fasting led to an inner conversation regarding my servitude for God, which would later lead to a local mission project too. It also paved the way for me to spiritually reset anytime I needed to. That next Sunday God would speak out loud to me and I was prepared to hear it.

Sunday August 19th, 2018

My first entry, "After today? Will it be different?"

This was one of the times I heard God's voice in my ear. It was clear and concise. When Erica was shying away from her water baptism. He said to me,

"Go before her as I have gone before you."

What God starts He finishes.

I believe that now.

I didn't before. I guess I landed in some sort of place where I believed maybe He got bored or frustrated with me. It wasn't until my fasting that I started accepting that Christ would love me no matter the sin. God views our sin and it is disregarded when you are born again. He doesn't hover over it. There isn't a time or place in some space between here and heaven when He "decides" your righteousness.

It doesn't work like that. When you have truly given your heart to Christ, it belongs to Him, right there in that moment. You will always feel His pull. You will always feel His affection to you, and you will always know you can cry out to Him in rejoice and in pain.

If you believe and you step out in faith, God will catch you every single time. It is when we confuse our human wants and needs with His needs that we can get thrown off our paths.

Our children are no strangers to these temptations either. That is why it is crucial to bring your child, offer them up to Father, and proclaim them as His children.

Wednesday, Prayer Meeting August 22nd, 2018

My prayer meetings start to fall off here. I had spent weeks at the alter praying and crying out for God to save my son. My knees would ache so badly sometimes when I came home on Wednesday because I would kneel at His alter for so long and just pray.

My entry reads, *"tired/frustrated/disappointed/but hopeful".*

Believe. Step out in faith and boldness. Bold prayers can flow out of a full heart.

> **Ephesians 3:20, "Now to him who is able to do far more abundantly than all that we ask or think, according to the power at work within us,".**

My walk up until this moment was both exhilarating and exhausting. I was feeling the pull of demons and feeling the strength of the Lord. That is something I have struggled with saying out loud until now.

Sometimes as a parent, especially as parents of teenagers, it seems like there is just constant evil waiting for them. And I think now I understand that might exactly be the case.

Being a teenager is one of the hardest times in a person's life. Had I come to terms that the battle was in fact raging behind my veil, I may have been able to save my children from some of their toughest issues. As far as the church goes, the importance lies in youth. It just does. If a church cannot sustain a youth group, they will not sustain in a community and are a limited congregation.

Something strange happened at this time in my life. I almost couldn't talk about it afterwards and it almost derailed my walk with Christ, momentarily, it might have. I was so angry and hurt.

The devils play for you once you have chosen Christ, is no joke. And here is why, because you CHOOSE to love God. Because you finally looked through the devil's smokescreen and are now helping those you know and love cross the Kingdom gates. I understand why some people in my life fought so hard for me to choose Christ, (Lindsey, Cindy *high fives all around*).

He truly does ease your burdens and provide a strength that is supernatural.

Chapter Seven
The Instant Message

<u>Saturday, August 18th, 2018</u>

Keep in mind I was waiting for a message from God. I was begging for a literal message from God. There was a feeling a few days prior to this incident that led me to say out loud to my husband that I felt like I would hear from our Pastor soon. He had asked me why, to which I had no answer. Simple mother's intuition maybe? I'm not even sure now.

What happened after my baptism is almost the opposite of what I thought would happen if I am being completely honest with you. I struggled with it. The internal battle was so intense it kept me out of church for a couple of weeks. I am embarrassed to say that my love for Christ wavered momentarily and I allowed the enemy to fill my heart with his putrid doubt.

Oh you read that right.

After I was baptized and I was on fire for Jesus, I stopped going to church.

I am an intensely intuitive person. It is something I've dealt with since I was a young girl. I wouldn't say prophetic, but intuitive. I could feel that God was going to send a message through our Pastor. I was certain of it. But I wasn't sure I wanted to hear it.

On a Saturday afternoon I was wandering through the local grocery like every other normal mom does. I was probably even wearing sweats and a messy bun.

Around 3:30 pm my phone made the dinging sound associated with social media messaging and I was not surprised when I saw that our Pastor had in fact, sent me a message. Yes! I knew he would reach out! I was anxious to hear what he had to say. Maybe it would be regarding our non-profit, maybe they needed me to volunteer, what could it be?

It wasn't much, to be honest. A simple greeting to which I responded with, "Thank you".

Then a message about needing to pray for my new-found faith in God, okay, a little more personal.

"I'll take all the prayers I can get, Pastor." I responded. That is great, I do need all the prayers I can get.

Then the kicker. A long drawn out message, riddled with talk to text typos, but seemingly personal and making more sense. The message is about my battle with the devil coming up soon. About rebuking him in prayer and that my faith needs to be the strongest it has ever been because the devil knows that God is after my heart and I am seeking God's heart.

He says my home needs a binding prayer. *(I don't understand a binding prayer!)* He starts typing out Bible verses from ***I COR-13:13*** and it is blaring in front of my face.

Here I am struggling, my personal life is hanging on by a weak thread, my soul is treading proverbial spiritual water, and I am reading, **"So now faith, hope, and love abide, these three; but the greatest of these is love."**

It's a home run. I rush home. I let my husband read the message. He can't explain it; I can't explain it. I am elated that God has literally typed out and sent me the message. I am convinced it is God.

Doubt starts to sink in. I can tell you it's like the frigid January type of cold.

At around 4:42 pm I send another message, "Is this really Pastor Lindell? I'm aware of the strain social media puts on personal interactions. I'm hoping the message was genuine. I can't imagine a church full of thousands of people you would reach out to me. However, I'll humor this and let you know the prayers are appreciated and very much needed. I've been on Satan's hit list for a few months now because of a path I chose to work with teenagers. It started with tragedy and hopefully will end in those very 3 things. Faith, love, and hope. Have a good evening Pastor it's on my heart that we meet soon."

NOTHING. The message gets read and no reply. Not a word.

I call my friend Lindsey. She tells me she thinks it's a scam.

I'm crushed but I keep reading through **I Corinthians**. I read about the gifts God gives us. I read about faith, love and hope. My eyes race back and forth between the text and the message and it all makes sense, how could this be a scam? Why would someone fake my Pastor's account and send me an unsettling and unnerving relatable message, a positive prayer message? I mean, hack an account and send scripture?

I comb over **The Way of Love and Prophecy** and **Tongues** the next two days.

Monday, I finally get someone to answer at the church. She tells me that it was a scam and apologizes. I try and tell her that no one asked me for anything, but she explains the account had asked others for money. I go in to copy and paste her the message and his responses are gone. Poof!

My heart was literally crushed. I didn't tell my husband, but I cried and cried, how could I get so mixed up in all of this? I was crushed beyond belief. I was played like a fool.

My prayer meeting August 22nd was the worst one yet, the pages prior to this proved that. I was emotionally spent. I was physically and mentally tired and I was angry at God. But I went anyways. I was so angry with Him that night. I don't know how I could even write out the word hopeful in my notes.

"*LOOK TO HIM*" is in all caps in my notes. *Believe. Step out in faith and boldness. Bold prayers flow out of a bold heart.*

How could God deceive me like this? How could He take His own word and use it to mock my heart? I had given Him everything. I had promised Him my children. My faithfulness. I was empty handed and sad.

I combed over the verses again. God says He will use your own language to communicate with you.

I didn't tell my friend Lindsey how disappointed I was to hear her logical explanation about the message. But I was so new to a mega-church, no one had warned me about something like this. The thoughts kept going through my head, how could that message be so applicable to my situation and it NOT come from God? After I begged Him to call to me during my fast? How could He? How could I have been so naïve?

I didn't return to church right away. I came up with excuses. I pulled away. I sulked like a defeated child.

Sunday September 16th*, 2018*

This Sunday was a game-changer for me.

God makes a fool of no one in His name. And what the enemy uses for evil, God will use for the Kingdom.

When I dusted off my humility and decided that my relationship with God was more important than the email debacle, I dragged our family back to church. They were probably suffering from some sort of Christian whiplash at this point. (You can laugh…)

My notes from that day are frantic and sort of illegible in my notebook.

They start with: ***II Cor.- 12:9 – "But he said to me, My grace is sufficient enough for you, for my power is made perfect in weakness. Therefore, I will boast all the more gladly of my weaknesses, so that the power of Christ may rest upon me."***

They flow to ***I Cor.-14:1-5 "Pursue love, and earnestly desire the spiritual gifts, especially that you may prophesy"***

> ***Luke 10:40 "But Martha was distracted with much serving. And she went up to him and said, Lord, do you not care that my sister has left me to serve alone?"***

Pastor was preaching regarding how the Lord has adopted us, how there is no condemnation in Christ.

You may think that this is meaningless, but for those of you who understand that God will speak to us in a way we might hear Him uniquely, it wouldn't be unreasonable to see that He could use something like a scam and take it, and make it better, make it His word. He wanted me to read those scriptures. He wanted me to take it to heart. The enemy had taken my feelings and used them against me, the enemy planted that doubt. But God used it for His goodness.

What makes this day in my life and our Pastors' life, (which he won't know until he reads this book), ironic and incredible, is that we had started a series on Romans 8:1. His sermon wasn't even directed in I Corinthians. He literally took a left turn from the sermon in Romans to I Corinthians.

He quoted and read the exact same message that had been sent to me from the false account. Word for word. Verse for verse.

I believe the Holy Spirit was speaking to me in that auditorium. I believe that God seized the opportunity to take the glory away from our enemy and use it to show me that it was indeed Him who reached out to me. I believe that He can use our modern world to reach us. I believe He humbled me and quietly reminded me to walk with Him in blind faith, never doubting His love or messages for me. You must believe God when He shows Himself to you. There isn't any other explanation as to how and why Pastor went off his notes and spoke directly to me. That is our supernatural God.

The next part of our story dives a little deeper into the strange message I had received. If you don't believe our God is supernatural now, you will after I tell you how that message tied into the next two or three weeks of our life.

My husband and I had planned a very small trip out of town for our anniversary. It wasn't very far, but it was a much-needed escape from our life here. We desperately needed a break. The boys were draining us with their partying and worrying after our son had returned back home from Washington state. We were holding on so tightly to Tylor that the grip on William had slipped. The "littles" were suffering from our attentiveness to the older teenager's life struggles.

The ball had been dropped.

My husband recognized we needed to go away and so away we went.

The history of my anxiety diagnosis starts in August of 2017 after I started suffering neurological response issues to extreme anxiety after I left a job where myself and my family had been threatened. I was working for an employer who had been illegally employing immigrant workers and was threatened with our safety and my career reputation if I were to blow the whistle. I blew that whistle and suffered the consequences. Afterwards the anxiety crashed down upon me and has taken up permanent residence in my life.

I battled anxiety about leaving the house this time and it was difficult. Our spring trip had been a disaster because I couldn't cope with being away. And here we were attempting another one.

My trips outside of the house and my speaking engagements were getting harder and harder to cope with until I finally rescinded and started taking my medication regularly. My husband was going to force me to go out of town. Less than a year after Alex died, my own life was crashing down around me. My husband was scrambling to try and keep me from falling apart.

We expressed our concern to both boys.

They were under strict orders about who was allowed into our home and who was not.

I'm sure by now you know this doesn't end well.

It was our first hard core realistic slide back into the ugly world of drugs.

The boys and several friends purchased LSD, the LSD had been laced and one of our dearest teenagers who suffers from a bi-polar diagnosis had a break down in my basement.

Oh, the enemy had in fact taken the opportunity and infiltrated my home. The message proved, again, to have come directly from God. In fact, a warning to guard our home from Satan and his rage at our love for Christ was ringing very true.

We found out late Saturday afternoon. We came home Sunday. When we returned home, I had to throw away broken furniture, clean up urine out of the carpet and blood off our walls.

By Sunday evening the argument between Tylor and I had escalated and in anger I told him if he couldn't stay sober, he could leave.

He did.

Later I would learn that the LSD had not left his system.

I would encourage anyone reading this book to educate yourself on the effects of the types of drugs out there for your teenagers' sake. The detox stage can be difficult and dangerous to say the least.

The boys were broken. I was broken. I was weak and angry. There might not be words strong enough to describe my defeat on that day. Our anniversary was a mockery to the boys.

My son had packed his bags and left my home.

I dropped to my knees in my bedroom and began to pray. I cried and prayed out loud. I went into the bathroom and cursed God through clenched teeth. I cried out to Him that I couldn't take it anymore. I collapsed on my bedside and I heard God **command** me. *"Wipe your face, get up and go get him"*. He said it in a firm voice. How could he talk to me like this? I wiped my face in desperation and embarrassment and called my son because God told me too. If he slept on the streets what would happen to him? Should I not show him the grace that God has shown to me?

He was waiting at a gas station about 6 miles away. I hugged him and told him I loved him. My husband and I put him in the car and brought him home. The car ride was mostly silent.

Drugs are a true demonic force.

The next few days Tylor opened about the realities the boys had dealt with. I believe, and Tylor believes, the devil was in our basement. Possession is real and people who use drugs and struggle from untreated mental illness are at a higher risk and are at the devil's mercy. Demons do in fact, exist.

The instant message rang true. The devil had been in my home. He was after our family and God had warned me.

Instagram entry, September 11th, 2018

A face only a mother could love.

That expression flies as freely as a dove.

You held his face when he was a child, warm smiling, in a happy place.

You can remember her snuggled down into a pink blanket, her binky, tap tap tap lightly, in her comfortable space.

There were no traces of dirt or grime on his sweet hands and feet.

Her cute tiny dresses hung in the closet waiting to meet.

His first day of school dances in your head.

Remember how her little backpack was so red?

His football games and her dancing queen dress?

Remember those times, but now your heart races, can you feel the stress?

The night they stayed out too late. The night her car rammed the gate?

His loud drug induced outbursts pierced the household at night.

Her uncontrollable cries behind her door were so light.

Your sister saw it. The neighbor just shook his head. Your best friends from high school ignored you instead.

My friends and family must... just be embarrassed, is all I said.

It's a face only a mother could love. But that's not true.

You, and you, and even you have loved them too.

Open your eyes and open your heart. Reach out to them because that is where you start.

#breakthestigma #ozarksagainstopioids #417land #417nonprofit #amwriting #writer #amshooting #poetry #poetryinmotion #livelove #guesswhosback

Reach out to someone struggling today. Not later. Not tomorrow. But today. Reach out to your friends' kids, your nieces and nephews, your sisters and brothers, and your children.

Family doesn't just mean blood. Community's need your support.

Stop making people embarrassed to ask or talk about mental illness or drug addiction.

Stop shaming troubled students. Stop judging.

Be a part of the solution.

If you or someone you know needs help, please reach out today. Ozarks Teen Transition Program

Chapter Eight
True Salvation

Sunday September 23rd, 2018

Service from home.

They say that true salvation is when you can look at your life after salvation and truly see a difference. I can tell you that it is true. While some habits remain hard to break, your overall life IS just different.

October 25th, Today is day 296.

I keep re-reading what I wrote previously. I don't have my church notes with me right now. This is a prime example of my scatter-brained notes. I am sitting at our rec center while sissy has basketball practice. I can hear the spin class behind the wall to my left.

The music is loud and going **Boom! Boom! Boom!** through the walls. I took the spin class once. It was enough to know I probably won't do it again. My lady parts were sore for days and I couldn't for the life of me understand why I had attempted to try it in the first place.

"Up! Down! Up! Down!" The trainer is screaming.

To be honest my lady parts hurt just listening it now. But I need to be writing and this may be my only hour to get it done this week. I haven't been to the gym regularly since Alex died.

I don't blame the situation on that. But it is important right now for me to reflect how this has affected our lives. I feel the tug of my old self.

Who is that?

Who was my "old self"?

Who is your "old self"?

_____

_____

I don't think I can go back to my old self since salvation. I don't want to.

Today on day 296, I received a phone call that led me to be in worship practically all day. In song and in prayer as I completed each of my tasks. I cried on the phone and had to excuse my composure. I cried on the way to the boutique. I cried once I got to work. I literally fell to my knees as tears hit the cold concrete floor of my shop out of sheer humble gratitude for my God. I am in fact, going into mission work. And I am so excited!

There is something deep down that changes a person after salvation. The only thing you want to do is learn more and do more in Christ.

The thirst for heavenly knowledge will never be quenched until you reach the right hand of God.

It's why the Apostles were so passionate about the words of Jesus Christ.

You want to save everyone.

When I go back over some of my old blog posts when I was going through my second divorce and later, a very heated affair, I see where I was searching. God was speaking to me even then. But I couldn't call it what it was. I was too self-centered to cry out to God and let it be known that I was drowning in my own "spirituality". I would sit in a hot bath during those couple of years and just cry out to God. I would be in such despair and yet my pride wouldn't allow me to truly reach for God. I had still put a wall between us. I called it, "being spiritual". I didn't call it, Jesus. The difference is resounding.

When I was writing and pursuing photography, I was trying to write about it or snap a photo of it. I was trying to re-create it as opposed to simply living it myself. I was telling people about it without truly living it. I never said Jesus' name. I was trying to live it but not truly glorifying God and talking about what He was doing for me. I hid it in some sort of pagan fashion. But He did not forsake me.

He carried me through even when the worst things had happened to me. Jesus Christ wept with me. The Holy Spirit cried out to and for me to acknowledge it.

Finally, my brave spirit stepped forward and decided that I was enough for Gods perfect love.

He didn't want me to be skinnier or smarter or quieter. He wanted me to serve just the way He created me, terrible humor and all. I don't have to go to spin class for Him to love me. Maybe my cholesterol, but not His love or acceptance.

I'd be lying if I didn't tell you that this week hasn't been full of disappointments. I've learned that God uses some of our disappointments to direct us towards His work. But today's phone call was a message that I am in the right direction. I am now working on local mission work with a couple of amazing women.

It was just a few short months ago I was writing "missionary work?" in my sermon notebook.

I think new Christian women get frightened because they don't feel qualified or smart enough or "Jesus" enough.

I know I did. We must do a better job at reaching and teaching. We must reach out to each other. The new-ness is both scary and exciting, and yet over-whelming.

Are you nervous about your new life?

_____
_____
_____
_____

Seek scriptures to comfort you in Christ.

_____
_____
_____
_____
_____

This coincides with the fallout that happens when Satan steps into a new Christians life and says, "Oh yeah, where do you think you're going?". The last two weeks I attended a huge Christian women's conference and God just kept telling me to <u>*write the book, write the book, write the book*</u>.

Every single day since the conference He whispers it to me, sometimes over and over. He won't stop tapping me on the shoulder. So here I sit. Listening to women who will have sore crotches tomorrow spin their donut and coffee calories away and typing about Jesus, to you.

You who feels inexperienced.

The you who is struggling.

The you whose friends have stopped talking to her since announcing her relationship with the King.

The you who has quit smoking, or drinking, or using or practicing normalized promiscuity.

The you who is hurting and emotionally bruised and angry.

The you who was trying to fill the void with mediation, crystals, yoga or being trendy and "not-basic".

The you who sometimes wants to hide from the kids, or the PTA, or work.

The you who is drinking a glass of Moscato.

Don't give up.

I think a lot of established people of faith do not understand why a new Christian can struggle so much and why breaching that gap is what builds the stable and reliable bridge to God. Let's just face it, it's a lot easier to talk about sitting with a prostitute or a recovering addict as opposed to doing it. We learned all about stigmas as a family when Alex died, and my friends found out my son was using hard drugs. They stopped reaching out to me at all. The most important people, including some family, just disappeared and scoffed at our struggle. Sometimes it doesn't take one encounter with God, the church, or the Spirit to change a heart. It takes several.

Maybe even years or despairing situations later. Maybe it takes the sheer terror of the desperation of a death to force God's love into our heart.

He yearns for us to cry out to Him. It is so hard for a new Christian woman. I know how much you are hurting. I know how hard it is. But don't let go of the feeling of hope and love that He gives you. Do not stop short of your eternal salvation. Look past the temptations.

Do we have the internal drive to follow through and sit with the prostitute, the addict, or the alcoholic for the long haul, or are we just there for the "beginning" of their journey? Is the church just getting the proverbial spiritual high that comes with a salvation count? What about the woman who was just released from prison? What about the homeless who haven't showered or brushed their teeth in months? What happens six months after a kicking and screaming salvation of a sinner? Oh yes, I went there. It's okay to be scared that you can't do it. The beginning isn't as easy as it looks. But I promise that it will fill your soul.

Are you able to teach your teenage daughter to be a Christian and then turn her loose in high school and allow it to happen? The first time she tells you she stayed late at a party and drove a drunk friend home out of worry, did you ground her, or did you tell her you were proud of her? Did you hug the stuffing out of her and feel her exhaustion for a social scene that is so difficult we can't even process it as an adult in these times? I can feel the proverbial lump in your throat. I don't say it to judge you, I say it because we made the mistake of compartmentalizing our son's life and someone died.

It wasn't our fault, it wasn't our sons' fault, but we didn't help the situation by asking him to just "not hang out with bad influences". At times, we have all been a bad influence.

Are you able to truly allow your child to live like Jesus?

_____

_____

_____

_____

_____

One of the things I've spoken about this year as a parent is that we are so quick to post happy tales of our young elementary kids who share their sandwich with the "poor" kid, or they want to give their used toys away at Christmas. Then our kids get into junior high and we abandoned all that we taught them.

Suddenly, we don't want them to have anything to do with those kids who might be at risk. It's no longer cute. We encourage separation. We as adults start to compartmentalize them.

The question is how can we prevent this?

_____

_____

_____

And an even bigger question, why do we do it?

How do we help?

I will tell you.

We raise God's warriors. We let them pick their battles knowing we have armed them with the word of God. We can be so swept up in our own issues that we forget they too have their own calling and purpose. Also, they're own issues. That may be the simplest thing we don't see.

It works the same for adults. Once salvation occurs and the true shift happens as a new Christian, oftentimes we are humbled by our own faults. I know I was. You are now. But don't give up.

When I think of salvation, I think about the first time I was on an airplane. I was a young mom. I thought the display from the flight attendant was ridiculous regarding the oxygen mask. It wasn't years later until I realized the importance of self-care and self-love. Now I realize that salvation is exactly like that.

Put your oxygen mask on first. Otherwise, your entire family and those around you may perish. Once yours is secure, move to saving those around you.

Once true salvation occurs you kind of shift from a mode where you are focused on materialistic things, people, world views and rich politics. You move to a place where spiritual knowledge is all you crave. You realize the importance of God in your family. You see how self-centered and wicked the modern world is, and you funnel everything down to encounters with God.

Let that happen.

You realize if you have less you can go and learn more. Less does mean more. You realize that the Earth is beautiful but ostentatious and cruel because human hearts have made it that way.

Not God. Not Jesus. Not the Holy Spirit.

You see how important salvation into the Kingdom is. You'll do almost anything to experience it. Once you're truly saved you give up everything you knew for it. You are imperfectly and perfectly human.

Christians who have been Christians their entire lives may shun you. They may go quiet and dormant. They'll gawk and mock your new-found love of Christ and His love for you. But that isn't your fault or, to be honest, your problem. It is theirs.

Your circle may grow smaller for a while as the air is sucked out of toxic relationships. Your marriage may transform. Your children may give you pushback. But it is all gentle love.

Do your best in the beginning to just connect with God. Remember, you aren't going to church to connect with people right now, you're going to connect with Him, in His house, to hear His word, and do as He will ask you to do.

There is a war happening. There is a war on the daughters of the King. So much so that we are killing our babies in the womb. Abortion and addiction and promiscuity is abundant because we are seeking love.

Oh yes, there is a war happening.

But there is also a revival happening. Look up. Keep looking up. Look to Him and you will choose the right side. Be a part of the revival! Do not be afraid. He chose you because of who you are.

It's a revival that will wage an equal war on the enemy on your behalf. A revival that is reminding women of all ethnicities, all nations, all walks of life that there is power in being a woman of God.

That our God, the highest King of Kings has given us a seat at His table.

We can mold and shape the next generation of so-called feminist and remind them that there is no feminist without the word feminine, and that there is nothing more powerful than being a daughter in Christ. Once you accept the Father's adoption, your entire world will light up. Both with the fire from hell and the glorious light from heaven. The enemy will do his very best to keep you as his own. You'll do anything to save the daughters of this earthly world.

In Christ there is no oppression or fear.

Remember, Jesus Christ, the son of the God of the Universe has given you the armor OF God. We are then new in Christ. You are now living in salvation. **You ARE SAVED**. Your veil has been removed.

Today on day 296, you and I have been chosen.

Chapter Nine
The Prodigal Daughter &
The Wayward Child

<u>Tuesday October 30th, Day 301</u>

This week we closed the doors on the final days of the boutique dream that I've been nourishing for a few years now. It's been a bastard of a dream. Often tricking me into thinking I was going to make it succeed. I mean, surely bible quotes on weird China made cheap mumu type tops isn't what everyone wants to wear?

I read recently that people should fail publicly. Most cannot stomach that thought. But really if I don't, I'm just teaching my children to shove their nasty skeletons in the closet. Really, depending on how much square feet they'll be able to afford, that may not be the best example to give them. Then there's the part where I want them to chase their big, giant, beautiful dreams! And find a partner, like mine, who supports and loves them honestly.

What I want to say as we close our doors, I want to say to the girl. The girl who thinks she should be too quiet. Or have blonde hair or hates mermaid hair or stop wearing funny tee shirts or thinks her heels are too high, maybe she feels ugly...stop. Cashmere is still cashmere, despite the high price some may pay for it. Don't be too quiet. Don't worry if your high heels intimidate others, and please, keep rocking the skirt with the sequins, and don't EVER give up those broke in vintage cowboy boots!

The rest will continue to scoff at our "eff-rich kids" jerseys and we will continue to live a life full of color, fingernail polish that changes color and hilarious inappropriate tee shirts.

All while raising great kids and leading beautiful lives.

Thanks for supporting us #417land ...

We love our home. Keep an eye out. We aren't finished using that hashtag just yet.

2 Timothy sums up my sinful heart at that time.

"But understand this, that in the last days there will come times of difficulty. For people will be lovers of self, lovers of money, proud, arrogant, abusive, disobedient to their parents, ungrateful, unholy, heartless, unappeasable, slanderous, without self-control, brutal, not loving good, treacherous, reckless, swollen with conceit, lovers of pleasure rather than lovers of God, having the appearance of godliness, but denying its power. Avoid such people."
2 Timothy 3:1-5

That post was on September 3rd of 2017. A little over two months after that, I would find out just how important those "bible quotes" on everything would become. I feel shameful when I read it. But I know God went before me. He knew the storm that was brewing.

This post is a lesson in humility for me.

To be honest I wasn't done using that hashtag. I use it for our non-profit now. But the original post, my goodness how embarrassing! My disdain for all things that were "holy" and outselling my own boutique came from the same place that held my "wayward child" mentality.

My identity was and still is the rebel. Only now, it is a rebel against a world that is against Christ Jesus. It's why He fought so hard for me. It is why He fought for Paul. I can look back at my own sins and proclaim them to the world, shut the door of shame, and move forward. Not everyone can exist on the same playing field that I've stepped out on. God knows a tiny piece of my identity still lies in the sinning ways of the wayward child.

He dwells in the deepest part of my soul to help me come to terms with my sin and allow the grace to seep through.

God is "I AM".

This statement and verse had baffled me quite a bit during this journey. Until this week. He is I AM because He has always been here. He isn't going anywhere. He will not forsake you. The ways of the Earth are not the ways of Heaven.

"I am the Alpha and the Omega," says the Lord God, "who is and who was and who is to come, the Almighty." Rev. 1:8

I had a hard time coming to terms with the fact that God chose me to be a King's daughter. That through my sins, the worst of the worst, He still wanted me. He waited for me. I know they say that God doesn't shake His head at us as a parent to a child, but I've often wondered if that I were the one that He gave at least a tiny head nod to.

Your sanctification process will be slow. Mine is. I am a "head talker". I constantly doubt myself. I fall somewhere between a wild horse and one who can pick a rider. One rider. Everyone else is getting bucked off. If you've grown up in the country, you know exactly the horse I am talking about. The wild animal instinct is undeniably in my core of existence. I am a wild flower in a garden of roses. I can't help it.

Sanctification after salvation is the equivalent of allowing the King of Kings, the Lord Jesus Christ to essentially place the crown on your head.

He nods. You accept.

Then, be quiet. Be as still as the calmest waters. Be as quiet as a mouse.

You pray and worship and cry out to Him until your soul hears His voice. A still, small voice isn't talking about intuition, it is Jesus. The Bible is the way. The Holy Spirit is your chariot.

Today I pulled all the false idols from our home. Mostly Buddha, but I had crystals and chakra cleansing and meditation materials too. Our Pastor gave us an amazing lesson this week and explained why some things are just not conducive to your new-found Christian title. Prior to becoming a prodigal daughter, I convinced myself that these things had not affected my home, my family, or my children. I am now, forever convinced that they in fact, did. I filled my home up with their preconceived notion of earthly beauty. I did it because I loved the beautiful things here, so much.

Here on Earth.

Christ teaches us to look up. He teaches us there is an after-life filled with perfection.

If I had given my children the chance to learn about Jesus and the love He filled our hearts with, they would have a tuned internal compass. Do I believe we wouldn't have landed where we are with drugs, or Alex's death, or the other "things" that can happen in our life? No. Not now. But the compass would have already been in place. I do believe, that in God's healing and in Jesus Christ's name wayward children are brought home every single day.

Prior to accepting Christianity, I was able to look past the evils in other religions.

I somehow made an excuse for the violence or ridiculousness of Hinduism or Buddhism. I had an attitude that those positions in life were not affecting me so, an attitude of to each his own.

It doesn't work that way. Being a rebel child, a wayward daughter, I wanted to be the one who allowed it. I wanted to be someone who didn't want to be told what to do. Why would I worship a God who wanted me to be *"fearful"*?

Fear vs. fear.

I used to live in a place where I questioned how a God could who is supposed to be loving to want us to FEAR Him.

What I can tell you is that God's definition of fear, which is very clearly taken out of context in postmodern society and even some churches, is used to scare you away from God. Sanctification can be scary. But don't let that fear confuse you.

When Jesus Christ speaks of fear, it is a fear of disappointment. It is a fear of rejection. It is the same fear your children must cope with when they have done something wrong.

Much like verse,

"Whoever spares the rod hates his son, but he who loves him is diligent to discipline him."
Proverbs 13:24

Discipline is different than punishment. It's why we abhor abuse clothed in punishment. It's why we abhor violence against children. Our natural tendencies are to protect our children. The "rod" is God's love. Hold fast to this concept. It is the difference in fear vs. fear. And it is imperative to your relationship with the Holy Spirit.

Be careful, prodigal daughter, that you don't confuse the two. Because this is the key to the success of bringing your children to God. Children will turn away from what they have been told to fear. Much like our natural abhorrence to the above mentioned, children will abhor that fear. God's commandments are not "rules". They are their father's promise to them. It is their compass of conviction. When we place pressure on their religion as opposed to their relationship to Father God, they may turn away with imperfection. Because even children recognize shame and imperfection.

They may, much like you and I did, turn away because they did not understand or were not led properly to drink from the Lord's well. Much like there are false decorative wells that sit among the lawns of middle-class America, there are false teachings.

The Lord's well will never run dry, it will never be mockery or empty, and it will never provoke fear as we think it to be.

Last night I was so tired. I fight so hard to be silent. I am rarely the quiet type. Reflective, but never quiet.

I drew a hot bath. I am borderline obsessive with worship now.

During sanctification it may become that way for you. Hold fast to that internal need to understand and re-connect with the Lord.

I heard Him speak to me. He said, *"I am with you"*. I'm so deep into meditating on God's word that even in the tub, bath bomb, candles and all, I can't escape being in thought regarding our lives and our connections with Him. You will be too, that is how you know you've entered sanctification.

God says He is the ever-present Shepard.

In **Isaiah 41:10**, *"Fear not, for I am with you."* Every word? True.

This morning as I was cleaning out the Buddhas and the supernatural books, I heard Him speak again, "make room for more. Sell it all. Throw it away. I have more for you." There is more in Christ Jesus.

The things you have been clinging to, crystals, meditation books, pagan ritual, or false idols and talisman? You won't need them. You will start to fill up. Suddenly you realize that what you let into your life may have felt good in the beginning, but now, at the end, it made you weak and empty. You were still tired. Exhausted, in fact, with life.

They don't work because they are not holy.

A friend said to me after I was baptized, "He always comes after the one." She probably didn't realize how much that influenced me over the months. I struggled with daddy issues. Then I struggled with mommy issues. I self-destructed in my twenties, then again in my thirties, I've been heartbroken and abused, and I just had enough.

But there He was.

He was waiting for me. "Are you tired yet?" He asks.

What are you tired of?

_____
_____
_____

I think about Him waiting for me all these years and my eyes well up with tears. He turns my face to Him every time and does not forsake me. He has promised to deliver my family from pain, and I know He will.

"If a man has a hundred sheep and one of them wanders away, what will he do? Won't he leave the ninety-nine others on the hills and go out to search for the one that is lost? And if he finds it, I tell you the truth, he will rejoice over it more than over the ninety-nine that didn't wander away! In the same way, it is not my heavenly Father's will that even one of these little ones should perish."
Matthew 18:12-14 (NLT)

"So, Jesus told them this story: "If a man has a hundred sheep and one of them gets lost, what will he do? Won't he leave the ninety-nine others in the wilderness and go to search for the one that is lost until he finds it? And when he has found it, he will joyfully carry it home on his shoulders. When he arrives, he will call together his friends and neighbors, saying, 'Rejoice with me because I have found my lost sheep.' In the same way, there is more joy in heaven over one lost sinner who repents and returns to God than over ninety-nine others who are righteous and haven't strayed away!"
Luke 15:3-7 (NLT)

Jesus rejoices over your return to Him. He has been chasing you down your entire life. Rarely does a new Christian tell you they never felt the tug of Jesus when they were wayward. Even in the darkest hour He is there. Through addiction, through promiscuity, through abuse, He waits. Much like we do with our own children. Tough love doesn't work.

When you call out to Him, when you cry for Him, He is there. It's instantaneous because of His omnipresence.

Has there been a specific time when you felt God's calling in your life prior to salvation and sanctification?

How is this time different?

_____

_____

_____

You are a Proverbs 31 daughter of the King.

> "10 [b] *A wife of noble character who can find?*
> *She is worth far more than rubies.*
> 11 *Her husband has full confidence in her*
> *and lacks nothing of value.*
> 12 *She brings him good, not harm,*
> *all the days of her life.*
> 13 *She selects wool and flax*
> *and works with eager hands.*
> 14 *She is like the merchant ships,*
> *bringing her food from afar.*
> 15 *She gets up while it is still night;*
> *she provides food for her family*

and portions for her female servants.
¹⁶ She considers a field and buys it;
out of her earnings she plants a vineyard.
¹⁷ She sets about her work vigorously;
her arms are strong for her tasks.
¹⁸ She sees that her trading is profitable,
and her lamp does not go out at night.
¹⁹ In her hand she holds the distaff
and grasps the spindle with her fingers.
²⁰ She opens her arms to the poor
and extends her hands to the needy.
²¹ When it snows, she has no fear for her household;
for all of them are clothed in scarlet.
²² She makes coverings for her bed;
she is clothed in fine linen and purple.
²³ Her husband is respected at the city gate,
where he takes his seat among the elders of the land.
²⁴ She makes linen garments and sells them,
and supplies the merchants with sashes.
²⁵ She is clothed with strength and dignity;
she can laugh at the days to come.
²⁶ She speaks with wisdom,
and faithful instruction is on her tongue.
²⁷ She watches over the affairs of her household
and does not eat the bread of idleness.
²⁸ Her children arise and call her blessed;
her husband also, and he praises her:
²⁹ "Many women do noble things,
but you surpass them all."
³⁰ Charm is deceptive, and beauty is fleeting;
but a woman who fears the Lord is to be praised.

*³¹ Honor her for all that her hands have done,
and let her works bring her praise at the city gate." Prov.31:10-31*

I was excited to get into this chapter because you know I am talking to you. Not a proverbial you, but **_YOU_**.

I don't have to call you out by name because you already know.

I don't have to pick and list and name all your sins because only you and God know.

I don't have to judge you. I don't have to yell at you. I don't have to force it on you. I just want you to know that I know how you feel. I know your heart. I have felt what you are feeling right now. As a mom. As a woman. As a chosen daughter of God.

Because you and I both know it's already there. Once God's calling is activated in your heart there is no denying His existence. Learn the stories of all the women in the Bible. They will change your perspective and your heart.

You will give everything you have just to serve Jesus Christ, the son of God. You will give Him your children. You will give Him your heart. Your family and friends may be pruned, and you will find yourself serving in the house of the Lord or serving on a mission to be close to new sisters. Your calling will be there. It always has been.

"In the same way, I tell you, there is rejoicing in the presence of the angels of God over one sinner who repents." Luke 15:10

Rejoice wayward child, because you are home. Your children are home. You are no longer lost. Shut out the world and just allow His presence to sink into your life.

Chapter Ten
Revival

The revival is up to us. When you're ready you will push forward a revival among your friends and family. The ground will move under your feet. With one foot in front of the other you will walk forward with Christ in you, and you in Him.

Some of us may run. Some of us will move slower. But what I will tell you is do not look back.

God has everything you have ever wanted in the now. Live in the now. For those of us who are damaged or fighting our own biological wayward children that is hard. In fact, it has been my most trying issue. I pray daily for the strength to simply focus on that day and how I can live in His love.

How can you apply Jesus' lessons to your present situation?

_____
_____
_____
_____
_____

How can you find time to worship?

_____
_____
_____
_____

How will you worship?

Some days it is simply a Christian radio station. Some days it may be a podcast. There are a lot of reading days for me. I read scripture in short bursts throughout my day.

There will be hard days.

To live in Christ doesn't mean your life on Earth suddenly becomes perfect. But I promise you if you give all Him to, He will heal your soul and will push you forward. He will walk through the hard days with you. Your soul is no longer alone.

He is the past. He is the present. He is the future. He is all knowing, and He always goes before us. Even before salvation He was before us. His grace is so deep and amazing it will transform you.

What I want you to understand is that all of us have bad days. The daughter of the King will have a past. She will be a sinner. She will be a saint. She will have good days. She will be fat, skinny, white, black, single or married. She will be tall and short, poor and rich. There is no label that keeps you from God. There is not a movie, music, or book that is keeping you from God. While it isn't easy to throw away the things of the Earth, you'll do it. Mostly because it feels good to let it all go. More so because it feels amazing to just give it to God in exhaustion.

Your friends will either gawk with magnificence or joke in vain. They will either still speak to you and ask questions, or they will question your faith. They will remind you of your sins. They may even provoke you.

Let it go.

God will replace what wasn't good for your soul. He will fill your cup and you will find yourself feeling less and less guilty for choosing your salvation.

What sin can you replace with righteousness right now?

_____
_____
_____
_____

We, as women, remind each other of our sins. Jesus Christ doesn't do that.

Try your best to understand this. Try your best to fight the temptations. You will sin. We all sin. But the deciding factor in your salvation isn't the rest of us. It is your Lord, Jesus Christ, the Savior. Your sins are already paid for. You are washed clean in the blood of Christ. Jesus gave Himself up on the cross, He wanted to bear our sins, because He loved us so much.

Live in, and for Him. He loved you first.

Do not forget that it was a choice for Him. He has wanted you from the very beginning.

And now, here you are, seeking Him. Help the others. Bring them home from the wilderness. Or better yet, go into the wilderness with them. Shower them with love and patience and kindness. It will repair your broken heart.

2 Timothy 6:11-12 "But as for you, O man of God, flee these things. Pursue righteousness, godliness, faith, love, steadfastness, gentleness. Fight the good fight of the faith. Take hold of the eternal life to which you were called and about which you made the good confession in the presence of many witnesses."

Find the wayward. Seek the lost. Look for the prodigal children of God.

Who comes to mind that you may bring the word of God to?

_____

Cry out for them as He has for you.

Live your life in constant prayer and worship.

What is your favorite time of day to pray?

_____

Remember how imperfectly perfect you truly are to Him.

Following Christ isn't about being perfect. I'd love to end this book with some crazy good story about how I became a minister or am leading groups of women to God. But at the end of the day I am focusing on the simple.

I am focused on creating a simple ministry that reaches out to rural kids in need of basic items and the love of Christ. I am focused on my son's newfound sobriety. I am focused on learning the way of the church and weaving through the human politics of it all. I am focused on getting my children to church on Sunday through grumbling gripey-ish attitudes because they are middle schoolers.

I am struggling some days to make it to prayer meeting on time and I am fretting about over-complicating our busy schedule. You see, I am you. I am the young you and the older you. I am the mom and sister and community member who just wants to make it through the day without spilling some sort of liquid substance down into my cleavage and all over my shirt. I am the you who pries herself out of an exhausted state in the morning or crams sev-enteen measly minutes of devotional in before bedtime at night. I am learning how to pray and ask for what I want and for what God needs. I am learning to listen to his smaller voice that nudges me along. I am working on my spiritual maturity every single day.

Today is January 3rd, 2019. It's been 371 days since Alex died and our world changed so suddenly. It's been a year since I began my angry, painful, joyful, soulful journey with the Lord. It's been less than a year since I fell in love with Jesus. I spent December 28th in a fog. I cried and felt pain like it was yesterday. And I rejoiced in the person my son has grown to be.

I suppose it may always be that way because my compassion nev-er seems to dim when it comes to raw human pain. I want you to know that if you are suffering from a wayward child, I guess that...we do get better. But of course, all in God's timing. That is my only hope and promise for my own children. I must trust God whole-heartedly. I must live whole-heartedly. It is who He has cre-ated me to be.

As we move past our year, I want you to see what a miracle Alex was and how much we love him. Our non-profit is failing, and I am patiently waiting on God to set my next move before me. But I know, that as we work to create a ministry for youth, that God is moving mountains. I want you to know that Jesus is your relief.

Stay strong sister, you are a child of God.

He sees you.

He loves you.

He longs for you.

Lean into him and trust His way. You are a daughter of the highest king, your creator delights in every single part of you and your family. He has chosen you as an heir to the greatest gift of all, the unreturnable and relentless gifts of His grace, His mercy, and the salvation of your soul.

You should feel good about every choice you have made that led you to Him and the truth.

Chapter Eleven

2 Timothy 6:6 "God be with you."

Now what?

You've stumbled your way through finding a church. You've struggled with finding your calling and pleasing the church. And yet somehow at the end of the day, what most churches don't tend to is the yearning to feel not just close to God, but close to the church.

You took all the classes and personality tests. You have showed up when no one else has. You have scolded those members who in the beginning told you not to over-promise your time or commitment to the church only to get burned.

I've often wondered that if Jesus wandered through the doors of our church would he overturn the tables of books being sold or start knocking our coffees out of our hands as he shakes his head in disgust. In *Matthew 21:12-13 NIV, *^{12}* Jesus entered the temple courts and drove out all who were buying and selling there. He overturned the tables of the money changers and the benches of those selling doves.* ^{13} *"It is written," he said to them, "'My house will be called a house of prayer,'[a] but you are making it 'a den of robbers.'*

I don't know. But I know the pressing to please the church doesn't always look like the road to pleasing God.

I know how you feel. I know how deeply you have loved Jesus through this. You've seen Mary's love for Him, you understand the sacrifice He made so that you and I can live a free life.

You long to be with Him, it's a yearning an unsaved soul doesn't understand. And yet, now what?

Maybe you just told the church no. Maybe you just sent a text backing out of another volunteer gig that you really didn't feel called to do. Maybe you've heard a sermon that somehow made you feel like you're a bad "Christian" if you decided you were NOT going to change another stupid diaper in the stupid children's area because you KNOW it is not your stupid calling.

Maybe you're tired of being asked for money at every single event you attend.

Stop right there.

I want you to know that I know how you feel. I know how you've watched the "group" seem to lovingly sit on the stage and coo over God's love for you. I know how you've heard Him press into you telling you that you are NOT called to change diapers or serve coffee. I know how you've been shot down and made to feel so small in such a big place. But what I must tell you, may not be what you wanted to hear.

Don't leave your church. You go back in there and you look for Him.

Don't feel like you are not important. Do not take God's whispers for granted. Listen to what He is telling you. Don't be afraid to stand up and speak when the time comes or when someone asks you a question.

I am a firm believer that new members of a church often hold greater insight and greater power than the members who have remained there the longest. New Christians see things that the tenure doesn't see anymore. We were put under one roof to help each other, not to compete.

You were not made to fall through the cracks. You were not designed and intricately weaved by God's very own hand to bow out of whatever spotlight He has put you under. Your story is important. He did not pull you out of the fire to live disappointed in His house.

Think of all the stories in the Bible. They aren't centered around a building of brick and mortar. They pray in the woods and the wild. They pray at the water. They pray at alters made in the wilderness. They pray in their homes and on the streets. Very little is the emphasis on the church building. But you an always find Him there, too.

It will take some of us a little time to work through this. It may take your conscious to be a people (or a pastoral staff) pleaser to understand that, now that you are saved. YOU are the church. Tenure or seminary school doesn't save someone from sinning. Tenure or seminary school doesn't make your calling any less important. The sole purpose is to bring people to Christ and the best way to bring people to Christ is through your job, through your schools, through your interaction with normal everyday women and girls that cross your path. Sometimes staying in the confines of the squeaky-clean church elite can cloud your judgement of what God is searching for. Or more importantly, WHO God is searching for. God uses every single saved soul for His good and wonderful purpose. You also have to remember there is a reason that you are different from what people think the normal church attender looks like. That is what makes our churches so awesome!

God wants you to know how special you are. He wants you to seek Him when you are frustrated with the church, or politics, or your kids screaming in the back seat of the car on the way to service. He wants you to move into the altar and allow Him to use your situation and your status as His messenger to salvation. He wants people, all people, who cross your path to know how important you are. He doesn't want you to feel frustrated or unhappy.

I recently had lunch with a girlfriend. She's also a member of a mega church. It was enlightening to me to see another successful and capable woman to be so vulnerable and admit her frustration with her church. It's something we don't talk about. It is something we shy away from. But it isn't because we don't want to upset the church, it's because often we confuse God's will with the church's will to survive and get things done. We know we heard Him tell us what to do, and yet, we find ourselves in a position of not saying no so that we don't displease our leadership. Or even worse, believing that our words aren't important to our leadership. When you reach deep down and call to God in prayer, He will lead you to where you are supposed to be. That may look like filling out a survey, speaking up, or maybe you find yourself watching service online in your pajamas with tears in your eyes because you can't muster up the courage to go in to service. It happens. But pray and GET BACK TO CHURCH anyway. Allow God to remind you that He will sort out the injustice, or the annoyances, or the natural human instinct to outlead one another. Your church matters are truly in His hands and He will never let you fall when you lean into His word and guidance.

So, now what?

You find your tribe. You find your people. You set a positive example and you serve where you are called to serve. If that means stepping out into a public position alone, then do it. If that means writing the book, then do it. If that means you want to change stupid diapers in the stupid nursery, THEN DO IT. Also, you can laugh a little bit. Don't take everything so serious.

God will ask you to do hard things. But God's calling is always clear. I think that sometimes in order to hide the light God has shone upon our face we end up saying yes to something that overwhelms us or truly causes grief and that isn't what He called you into His arms for. You can say no to the church and yes to God. Your life and your circumstances are what He wants to use. God has a heart for those who simply want His heart. It truly is as simple as that.

I think the simplicity that is involved with salvation is something we overlook. And at the end of the day, I want to put my head on my pillow, and I want God to speak to me. I want Him to speak through me. I want Him to use the gifts He placed into my hands to reach women like you and pull you into His embrace. I want Him to use our circumstance and our story and make something beautiful out of it.

I want Him to use your story and I want your story to teach me something new about His living love for us.

1 Peter 1:22-24 NLV says:

> *[22] You have made your souls pure by obeying the truth through the Holy Spirit. This has given you a true love for the Christians. Let it be a true love from the heart. [23] You have been*

given a new birth. It was from a seed that cannot die. This new life is from the Word of God which lives forever. [24] *All people are like grass. Their greatness is like the flowers. The grass dries up and the flowers fall off.*

God uses each and every one of us in such a unique way that we can all learn from each other. Humility isn't just assigned to those who are seemingly below the self-righteous, it is assigned to us all. Your testimony is just as important as the next person's and He will use you. God will always finish what He has started.

I want you to know that I pray for you. I pray for your families and I pray for your circumstances.

Prayer saved my son. It saves families. I believe in prayer so much that it isn't just an internet worthy statement for me. It isn't an in-passing conversation. I believe that when He delivered you from your own personal hell on this Earth that He has shown you a better way. And even when we struggle with the earthly human pain or disappointment, He will bring us out of it if we allow Him to.

Philipians 1:6 NIV- *being confident of this, that he who began a good work in you will carry it on to completion until the day of Christ Jesus.*

Let Him finish what He started in you.

God bless and stay true to who He has created you to be.

365 days with God turned into an eternity with the One who has created me. I pray it is the same for you.